Ty's Story

Ty's Story

A TRUE STORY ABOUT LIVING WITH BEHCET'S DISEASE AND THE AFTERLIFE

§

A mother's undying love to find the answers she
so desperately needed to go on

Vicki Hamm

ISBN: 1530104882
ISBN 13: 9781530104888

This book is dedicated to my son,

Ty Michael Fritzsching

August 5, 1980—October 12, 2009

Acknowledgments and Special Thanks

§

I WOULD LIKE TO THANK my two beautiful daughters, Chanti and Kareen, who are a blessing to me and have helped me through this difficult time in my life. They both have busy lives with husbands and children, but they have always been here for me when I needed them the most. I am grateful for their love and support. I don't know that I could have moved on without their continued love and support.

I also would like to thank Sarah C., who was there for Ty in his darkest hour when he needed a special friend. She brought love and hope back into his life when he was alone and in unbearable pain.

Thank you to Jess A., who Ty met when his friends had all turned away from him during his dark days. Jess was there for Ty and believed in him. Just like Sarah, he understood the pain Ty was going through even though they did not understand why, but then again, doctors could not understand why. Jess and Ty both wrote and played beautiful music together, which temporarily kept Ty's mind off his pain. So sad they could not have continued, as they had great plans for their future.

Thank you to my husband, Marc. He has been a wonderful father and grandfather to all five of our beautiful grandchildren: Cody, Isaac, Daly, and our two granddaughters, Maci and Satori. Ty never met Satori. Without Marc's love and support, I would never have wanted to go on with my life. He is my rock. He understands me like no one else in this "place."

A Very Special Thanks to Marti Tote

WITHOUT MARTI, I COULD NOT have written this book. Marti asked me one day if I could write *Ty's Story*. That was the last thing I thought about doing, as I didn't consider myself a writer! I believe Ty needed his story to be told, and Marti brought that to my attention. Thank you, my dear friend. You are such an inspiration to me. Ty has brought us together for a purpose. I am so thankful for everything I have learned from you and continue to learn from you. You have such a wonderful gift, and you have brought my son to me. It does not get better than this!

I never knew how I felt about death until I lost my son. Ty has shown me repeatedly he is still with me. When you die, you leave your physical body, but you live on with your same personal traits and personality in the form of energy. If you are one of the many who can connect with our loved one's energy, you can communicate with that loved one. It is almost unimaginable, but when it happens, it is beautiful and so very special. Our loved ones leave us special signs; we just need to be open to them when they give us these signs. I feel very fortunate because Ty leaves me signs daily in many different forms.

I no longer fear death as I did as a child and know now that when you leave this place called earth there is no real death, as you live on in the form of energy.

Marti, you are one special lady, and I will forever be grateful to you for bringing me my son and my many family members who have passed on. I will love you always, my friend.

Note: Marti Tote is a medium, psychic, and life coach who lives in Reno, Nevada. Books written by Marti:

When It's Time to Say Good-Bye
A Whisper in the Wings

PART I

Many Changes Are Coming Our Way

§

AFTER HAVING GROWN UP IN the Los Angeles area, I was so very happy to have the opportunity to move to Atascadero, California. Atascadero is a small town on the Central Coast of California, halfway between Los Angeles and San Francisco. I moved to Atascadero with my daughter Chanti and my husband at the time. As long as I can remember, I always wanted to live in the mountains and nearby lakes. Even as a child, I remember hating North Hollywood, a suburb of Los Angeles, with its old cracked cement sidewalks. I never felt like I belonged there for some reason. I hated the smog, the traffic was horrible even back then, and the people were unfriendly for the most part. I remember as a small child, I would beg my parents to please move our family somewhere out of there where there were mountains, trees, and lakes. It was almost as if the mountains were calling to me to come to them. My parents would always tell me we could not move because their jobs were in the Los Angeles area. At the time, I did not understand this. I only wanted to be somewhere beautiful, where I could feel at peace.

Growing up, I lived in North Hollywood with both my parents, my two brothers, Gary and Jon, and my sister, Jan. My sister and younger brother, Jon, are twins. I remember everyone in North Hollywood was always in such a hurry, and they never stopped to smell the roses, including our family. Neighbors hardly knew one another or spoke. I remember having a next-door neighbor whom I named Mamie when I was a young child. She was like a mother to me, though much older than my mother. She was more like a grandmother. I saw Mamie almost every day when I was growing up. She would work in her garden or clean her house, and I would come over and talk with her. My mother was always at work and not home so much when I was growing up. I loved Mamie very much and confided in her. Whenever I had a difficult time at home, I went to Mamie and talked to her about it. She was a Catholic and a retired nurse, so she was always at home. While nursing, Mamie met Alice, who was one of her patients, and they became friends. Ironically, Mamie's name is "Alice." Alice needed home care, so Mamie moved her into her home that happened to be next door to our house. She got the best of care. As long as I can remember, Alice, for the most part, stayed in bed, as she was very ill. For some time, I went to church with both Mamie and Alice, when she was up to it. I was around ten years old at the time. The last time I saw Mamie I was seventeen, and she passed shortly after that. Alice had preceded her in death.

After my husband, Chanti and I moved to Atascadero, California, I didn't keep in touch with too many of my friends from the North Hollywood area. It seemed people just went their own way, and I went mine. From time to time, I would think about certain people, but then I would forget about them and tell myself that they moved on and I should do the same.

I loved living in San Luis Obispo County, as it had so much to offer in terms of my peace of mind and the beauty of the area. This was a great change from where I grew up. I was so happy to be able to move my daughter out of the city and into a smaller community. I had a good job I liked with the City of San Luis Obispo Police Department. I worked in the Records Department where I transcribed police reports and kept monthly statistical information regarding crimes in the city. I worked about eighteen miles south from Atascadero, where we lived. Marc worked as a machinist 12 miles north from Atascadero. It was a much different life there compared to what I experienced growing up. I loved looking at the cows and small rolling hills on my way to work every morning as opposed to crowded freeways and angry people cutting you off the road, as they were late for work. I finally felt like I had found some countryside that I had longed for my whole life; I felt like I belonged there, that this was my home. The people appeared to be friendlier and nicer, and there was just a good feeling about being there.

While working for the City of San Luis Obispo, a few of us would often walk downtown, which was just a couple of blocks away, and we'd order our lunch. I will never forget the first time I walked into Muzios, a delicatessen and wine shop, and when I did not have enough money to pay for what I wanted to purchase, they placed my bill on a tab. They just asked me where I worked, they wanted my phone number, and they said I could pay for it later. That for sure was a new one on me! The town was pretty low-key back then. The year was 1978. Life was simple then. That would never have happened in North Hollywood where I grew up.

Time passed, and my son, Ty, was born in August of 1980. This was a very special time for me. I had a daughter and now a son, and I was very happy, though not so much in my marriage.

My life was busy. I worked full time and took care of two small children, so I did not see my family, all of whom were down in the North Hollywood area of Los Angeles, as much as I would have liked. My father would bring my mother up to see the kids and me about once a month. They often brought my grandparents, Nanie and Papa, to visit. We loved having all of them come up, and we would have a wonderful time making a big meal for everyone and just hanging out with family. Those were happy times for all of us.

I did not see much of my younger brother, Jon, or his twin sister, Jan, during this time. For as long as I can remember, Jan was not well and could only travel up to Atascadero to see me a couple of times. My brother, Gary, and I remained very close and talked on the telephone every week. It was always great talking to Gary. He and his wife, Cindy, came up to see me when they could. As a family, we were together almost every holiday and birthday, unless something unforeseen got in the way. We loved getting together for barbecuing, taking trips to the lake, and just hanging out together listening to music. I will always treasure those times with my family.

It was not too long after this time that we received the terrible news that my father needed surgery because he had a brain tumor. My poor father had suffered from incredible migraines and ringing in his ears for a long time, but we never expected this. We finally had answers, and he was getting help. We were optimistic about his recovery, as he was only fifty-eight years old at the time.

My father never woke up from his brain surgery. During the time my dad was in his coma, I was working. Family members called me to say I needed to come down to UCLA Medical Center immediately to see my father, as they did not think he would make it through another day. This happened on many occasions, and it was a very difficult time for all of us. I lived several hours away from the rest of the family, and it was beginning to take a toll on me. We would talk to my father when we saw him, and we saw movement in various parts of his body at times, so we truly believed he would wake up eventually. My father and mother both worked at UCLA Medical Center. It was ironic that my dad, an electronic technician, fixed the machines he was hooked up to while he was in a coma. I don't remember my father ever going to see a doctor before this time, as he never got sick and did not believe in them, for the most part.

After my father had been in his coma for eighty-nine days, numerous doctors told us there was no hope that he'd ever wake up from his coma. The brain stem had disconnected from his brain, and there was no chance for recovery. We had him taken off life support at this time. This was a very sad time for all of us.

Unfortunately, my father had been misdiagnosed for six years and he died at Thanksgiving 1982. He had complained of headaches and dizziness, and he would fall asleep at the drop of the hat! We would all go out to eat, and he would just fall asleep in the middle of dinner. It was weird. We had no idea whatsoever he was sick because the doctors told him there was nothing wrong. They told him that the ringing in his ears was from his being a ham radio operator for all these years. When I think back, we would laugh at him for being so silly as to fall asleep like that. We had no idea how sick he was. He didn't really believe in doctors to begin with. Then, when he finally went to see doctors for help, they failed him in the end. We were all very sad.

I was very close to my father and I took his death very hard. My father's death changed the whole dynamics of our family. I do not think our family was ever quite the same after my dad's passing. We would still get together at holidays and such, but I never felt like it was the same without him.

It was not too long after my father passed away that my husband and I got a divorce. This was an extremely difficult time for me, raising two young children on my own and working full time. I was living in Atascadero, with my family living in Los Angeles, about three hours away. I felt alone. I looked forward to my calls from my brother Gary every week, and we would talk for hours about everything. He was my rock!

My children made me strong through my experience as a single parent. I was so glad to have them and did the best job I could as their mother.

Chanti was very outgoing and continued to grow, enjoying her dance and music, and had many friends. Chanti was involved with everything in school and was very popular. I went to many performances for her plays, violin lessons, jazz dance classes, and ballet activities.

Ty was not as outgoing as Chanti. He was involved in a few plays at school. For the most part, Ty would play quietly for hours in his room by himself or with his sister. He would build things with Legos or Balsalite, or draw pictures of nearby houses in the neighborhood. Ty was good at soccer, but he seemed to like to play alone more than participate in organized sports. He did not have loads of friends like Chanti, but he seemed to be very content being home or going wherever I took him. Ty was not like younger boys; he was subdued and a deep thinker, yet he had a fun, mischievous side to him, which he liked to show his sister when I was not home.

I met my future husband, Marc, when Ty was about three years old and Chanti was nine years old. Marc had a daughter, Kareen (Kari), who was two years old at the time. Ty was so young he did not care that someone new had come into his life, and it was an easy transition for him.

Marc had to win Chanti over. It took him time, and he was patient. Marc had grown up with an overbearing stepfather who threw himself at him trying to be his dad, and Marc swore up and down he would not do that to a kid, as he resented his stepfather for that. It paid off in the end, as Chanti adored her stepfather and Ty did so also. I remember a time though in Home Depot when someone walked up to Marc and said what a cute son he had, and Ty said, "That's not my dad." It's funny, looking back at this now, as Marc was always there for him, and when Ty got older he introduced Marc to his friends, teachers, or whomever as "my dad, Marc."

Marc and I were married after about a year of getting to know one another and figuring out that we felt like we were soul mates. If you believe in love at first sight, this was it. It sounds corny, but there's no other way to explain it. Marc treated my children as if they were his, and I did the same with his daughter, Kari. We bought a house and moved in together. Yes, we bought the house, and we got married afterward. My mother may have had a little part in that! She did not think any mother raising children should live on her own.

Kari would come to stay with us, and we would take her on vacations as often as we could have such visitations. The transition for Kari was the hardest of the three children, as she did not quite understand all that was happening to her. All the kids got along well and life was good for us, though sometimes hectic. There were times when Marc and I would hear Ty and Kari talking alone in another room, not knowing we could hear them. They would be talking about their mother and father and who belonged to whom! It was funny when I think back, as they probably had it more together than all of us as parents.

Atascadero was a small town of approximately twenty-five thousand people at the time and a very nice place to live. Our children were very active in sports, dance, and all the activities that children enjoy. We were always busy. The kids were coming and going, and we tried to get all three together when we shared special outings together.

All three of our kids were very well behaved, which made it easy for us to take them wherever we went—taking them to our friends' homes for barbecues, to the lake boating, to events at the parks, or anywhere else we wanted to go. We even purchased a boat and went to the lake every weekend with our good friends to barbecue at the lake with their kids and family members. There was always a crowd, and everyone had fun.

A Visit from My Father

In 1987, my father came to me for the first time after his passing. I had had surgery and was at home recuperating. We were living in Atascadero, and I was lying awake in bed resting, when my father appeared to me as plain as can be, as it was daylight. He was at the foot of the bed and told me I was going to be all right. I was not afraid, as this was a very comforting visit. I did not want this visit from him to end, as I did not want him to leave me again.

I was so excited about what had transpired that I had to tell my family, especially my older brother, Gary, who thought I had lost my mind when I told him, as there is no way I could have had a visit from our father who had passed. I was so very disappointed with him not believing me, as I just wanted to share with the world what I had experienced. To me it was a miracle, and I was so excited.

After that, I just kept this experience to myself. Something changed in our family after my father's passing, leaving us further apart than ever.

He never appeared to me in his physical form again until September 11, 2014.

§

As a small child, I remember Ty being somewhat quirky. He had this thing about wearing the same blue shirt and blue pants to school every day of the week. I would lay his clothes out the night before he went to school, and the next morning when I went into his room to wake him up, he would be wearing the same blue pants and blue shirt I had placed in his dirty-clothes basket the night before. He would pull them out of the dirty-clothes basket and put the clothes I laid out for him back into his dresser drawer. It was a crazy thing with him that I never figured out. He could have worn this same outfit as a uniform every day of the week to school and been happy with that. I guess I should have bought him a set of the same clothes for every day of the week to wear to school. It would have alleviated many arguments we had each morning. Evidently, he was stressed about what he was going to wear. He eventually outgrew this—thank goodness. As he got older, he loved to dress up. I was so glad for that.

When we had a holiday with the family, Ty would walk out as if he was dressed to go to a wedding. He loved dressing up but was very particular about what he was going to put on to wear. He did not care if he was overdressed. He had very good taste in clothes as he got older, and the girls loved it.

In 1991, we moved from Atascadero, California, to Reno, Nevada. We moved because Marc lost his job and could not find work in the area. We decided a change would be good for all of us, so we decided it was time to move on.

We looked in California, Oregon, Idaho, and Nevada. By this time, I was feeling burned out in my job in San Luis Obispo after thirteen-plus years doing the same thing, so we went for it. I went with Marc to Oregon for a job interview, and then he went to another interview in Nevada.

We fell in love with Reno, Nevada, and this is where we ended up moving. This was a good move for Ty. Ty was to start middle school, and Chanti went to Italy as a foreign exchange student. This was an exciting time—new house, new jobs, and new area. Marc had gotten a job as a machinist making parts mainly for slot machines. I started work as a legal secretary with the District Attorney's Office in Washoe County. Everything was new for us.

Reno was a lot bigger than the town we had come from, and it had so much more to offer. We actually had stores and shopping here and did not have to drive for two hours to get to a decent store to shop. The three of us were very excited about our move and new venture. Also, we were going to live in the snow for the first time and have four seasons. We had so many lakes for water skiing, exploring, and fishing. Many changes were going to take place.

After our move, Ty had quite a transition in school. Ty was always a small child, wore glasses at four years old, and had braces. People made fun of him, and he was kind of a loner. He was a very sweet, sensitive kid, and most of his friends when he was younger were girls. When we first moved to Reno, Ty made some friends, but he also got into many fights because he was smaller than kids his age, and he was picked on quite often.

At one point, after living in Reno for some time, Ty had gotten himself into trouble with another child. I grounded him and told him he could not use the phone, watch television, or have any friends over for two weeks. Ty had met an older boy who came into our home while we were at work and charged numerous toll calls to our phone. I was mad, and Ty knew it! That never happened again.

While Ty was grounded, I offered him my guitar and said he was allowed to play it if he wanted. He did not seem interested in the least at the time. I figured

I would give it to him anyway, as both his uncles and his father played music. I figured, who knows? One week later, he came to me and said he wanted guitar lessons. The funny thing was that I never saw him pick it up to play. He must have played around on the guitar while we were at work. I took him to Jeff at Bizarre Guitar for lessons. Ty went to Jeff for about a year, and finally Jeff said he could not teach him any more than he already knew.

Ty remained friends with his guitar teacher over the years and continued to play music and teach himself everything he could. He learned to read music and studied music history in school. He also started playing the piano. We had a piano and an organ at home, and Ty played both of them for hours. It was amazing how easily music came to him. Ty played guitar in numerous garage bands over the years, starting at the age of thirteen. The kids would play music at our house several times a week and occasionally elsewhere. They would also play all-age shows at the YMCA. As his music evolved and he got better, he started playing at different halls and all-age shows around town. They also played at the skate park.

One of his very first bands, a "straight-edge band" called "UnConquered," had planned to go back East for a couple of weeks and wanted Ty to play guitar for them. As these guys were all older than Ty and they were of legal age, they came to our house to meet us. Ty was sixteen at the time. It was crazy, as all these men in their twenties came to our house. I felt like Marc and I were doing an interview before we let our son take off on a wild adventure! Geez, I even wrote a note to the oldest in the band that he had the authority to take care of Ty in the event of a problem while on the road—wow. Was I crazy, maybe? But, I liked these guys. With Ty being under age, I felt pretty good about these guys, as they did not drink alcohol or do drugs, as it was against their beliefs given their commitment to being straight edge.

Ty toured with UnConquered at the age of sixteen and then again at seventeen, all over the United States. He would call me during his travels so excited and tell me what was going on and what their shows were like. Some nights they played for thousands of fans. I remember being awakened in the middle of the night after Ty had played a show in Baltimore. He played with some big-name bands there. When they started to play, he said he suddenly saw their band on a large screen behind them, which they did not expect. They all thought they had hit the big time! It was so much fun for them, and it was great to hear Ty's excitement in his voice. He was so young and having the time of his life. Marc and I felt their excitement right along with all of them. They would not make much money along the way, so they lived out of a van for the most part or would find a place to camp. They didn't care if they made a lot of money. They were happy if they made enough to pay for the gasoline in their van and maybe pay for some food. They just wanted to play music. I think many a times they lived off Top Ramen noodles, but they did not care as long as there was music to be played.

The boys played in Pennsylvania, and my very dear friend Gloria, with whom I grew up and went to high school in Southern California, lives there with her husband. I told her that UnConquered was playing in her vicinity, and she went to see them play. She had never met Ty before this. That night the whole band stayed overnight at her house, and all I could think about that evening was that her husband must be one special guy to allow all these strange men to stay at their home. I am so glad my friends were able to meet our son, as they are so special to me.

That's exactly what it was—an adventure. I remember Ty telling us later how thankful he was that Marc and I allowed him these experiences that he would never forget. He went to Washington, DC, and he saw things he would never have seen had it not been for these road trips with the band. These guys were around us often and were like family to us.

Ty had several friends during this time in different bands. He went to see them play their shows, and they came to see him play. Marc and I were always going to these shows, and everyone looked forward to us coming. Usually at least three bands played, and the music started at 11:30 or 12:30 and continued until 2:30 in the morning. The later the music started, the better the band was.

Marc and I could not stay up that late, as we had to work, so we would take a nap early in the evening, and Ty would call and wake us up around 11:30 or so. We would get ready to go out and meet him where he was playing right before they were to go on stage.

Life was never dull when Ty was around. Ty was still getting into fights at school from time to time. At one point, I told Ty to never start a fight, but if someone were to hit him, he was to stand up for himself. Then I proceeded to tell him a story about when I was in sixth grade.

I was very shy and introverted and would walk to and from school about two miles each way every day by myself. Two sisters, Tara and Kim, lived down the street from me. Tara was a year younger than Kim and me. They would follow me home from school each day, make fun of me, and hit me with their lunch pails. I never used a lunch pail, only a brown-bag lunch. They would always pick on me when there was a group of them by their side. I don't know why they didn't like me and why they picked on me, other than that I was shy and a loner and they were in a group. This abuse went on for some time, until I finally could not handle it any longer.

After school one day, I got up the courage to walk over to Tara and Kim's house and knock on their door. They lived about a half block down the street from me. Tara answered the door, and I asked her if I could speak with Kim. Kim then came outside, and I beat the crap out of her. Little meek me did that, yep! They never bothered me again. Unfortunately, it took standing up for myself for the abuse to stop. I never had a problem with these girls or anybody else again. Suddenly, Miss Shy Girl at school was more popular, and everyone thought I was cool. Funny how kids think.

To get back to Ty's story. Some kid at school picked a fight with him, and he defended himself and fought back. Ty was suspended for three days from school. The principal of the high school called me in to talk with him. I was furious. I told the principal that he might as well have suspended me. I was the one who told Ty to fight back if someone picked on him. We got nowhere on this one. Both Ty and the other kid were suspended. Geez, life was sure interesting in those days.

Ty would sometimes be out at a show, and I would get a call from one of his best friends Nate. Marc and I would be sleeping, and the conversation would go something like this. "Vicki, don't be alarmed, which hospital can I take Ty to?" Geez, how do you not get alarmed when being awakened with a question like that? Ty was always getting hurt with silly stupid things. His friends looked out for him though.

All the UnConquered guys were big guys and were very muscular. They had tattoos all over their bodies and had many body piercings. It was about this time that Ty starting working out at a local gym. His body really started changing, and he had muscles and this incredible physique. Girls loved him. Boys from the high school tried to fight Ty, as they were jealous of him and thought he was a pretty boy. To top things off, Ty played guitar, and the girls loved the fact that he played in a band. He was a screwball on stage. The girls loved it when he wore his, what he called, wifebeater T-shirts while on stage, and then he'd take it off! This was when Ty really started to grow up and realize whom he could trust and whom he could not.

Ty then went on to college, and he was thinking that he would like to go to chiropractic school one day. Though he wanted to be a full-time musician, he knew the odds of that happening were slim, and he needed a backup plan. He was a smart young man and got good grades without having to study very hard. He worked for a short time at the gym as a trainer. It was hard for him to get his own clients, as the people already training there had worked there for years, but he still tried. He loved training. During this same time, Ty was asked by the university if he would tutor other students in physics and math. Ty did so and enjoyed this very much.

He was so much fun to be around. Ty was a funny guy and could make you laugh. Ty had many girlfriends and good male friends. He had become very popular, and he was handsome and talented! Ty was in his element and happiest when he had a special girlfriend, but he kept special bonds with several of his other female friends over the years.

Chanti came back from her foreign exchange student travel, moved to Lodi, California, and married. She and Ty remained extremely close. Ty came to Lodi, and Chanti came up to Reno all the time for Ty's shows with his band. Many times Chanti would bring friends with her to Reno to see Ty's shows when he was playing.

On one occasion, the band he was in at the time, Steve Dave, played a surprise party for Chanti's twenty-eighth birthday at her friend Mieke's house in Lodi. The band drove down to Lodi, and I remember Chanti was so surprised and a bit overwhelmed by this at first. The band played music inside a room by the pool area. We had a barbecue, drank wine, and went swimming. Everyone had such a great time that day.

Steve Dave sometimes played in Lodi at local bars when we were all together and just had fun. Sometimes only a few people would show up for their shows, and at other times the places they played would be packed. They never knew what to expect nor did they care much as long as they could play music.

Ty and Chanti had a special bond and were best friends. Over the years, Chanti and her friends attended many of Ty's performances with various bands, even on the East coast. Marc and I went to every show where Ty ever performed unless we had been sick or if the show had been too far away. I think we were the only parents who ever attended the shows. We loved it, and Ty's friends were like our kids and family. If we didn't show up for a performance, band members asked where Mom and Dad were. This had become our life, and Ty's friends were ours.

Ty's life was music. He lived and dreamed music. We would sit for hours listening to music with him, or he would play music for us. We were his audience. Our house was always open to his friends, and they often used our house for band practice. Later, they rented space for their band practice. Ty still asked Marc and me to come to his practice sessions. We were all so very close. Chanti was always planning her next trip to Reno to see a show with Ty in whatever band he was in at the time.

Unfortunately, Kari missed a lot of these shows that Ty was in. She had a tough childhood, with her mother moving her all over the country. We were lucky to see her when we did and treasured those times. Kari, Ty, and Chanti were very close regardless, and Kari and Chanti remain close.

Ty also loved to cook, and he would make dinner for Marc and me to surprise us. He could make something out of nothing! I would look in the pantry and see nothing that I could make to eat. Ty would look, and the next thing I knew, he had made us this fabulous meal. When Ty was traveling with the band UnConquered, they were vegans, and Ty learned how to cook during that time. I sure love men who can cook! Also, Ty did not drink until he became twenty-one years old. UnConquered was considered a straightedge band that did not believe in drugs, alcohol, or sex unless it was within a serious relationship.

The three of us would sit around on Sunday afternoons watching a movie, eating snacks, and just enjoying the day. Sundays were a special time for us, as the three of us always sat down as a family to eat dinner together, drink wine, and talk for hours about life. Ty always had a lot to say, and I loved listening to him. We always looked forward to these times.

When we were having friends over for the evening, I would always ask Ty to pick out our music for the evening. He would ask who was coming, and depending on who it was, he would pick out our music for that evening. He always had the perfect CDs picked out for us. If anyone knew music, he did. Then, when our friends arrived, Ty would come out and join us for dinner, wine, and conversation, and he would enjoy the evening with us. It always amazed our friends that Ty was so unlike other young men his age, that he enjoyed being with us and not rushing to go out with his own friends.

We had a boat, and the three of us went to the lake every weekend. Our favorite place was Lake Pyramid, as the water was warm and it was great for water skiing. Ty was our captain and loved to drive the boat. We'd go out for hours just hanging out in the boat, listening to music, talking, drinking wine, reading, and swimming. It was so relaxing. We would just hang out in the middle of the lake, and it was beautiful. We wouldn't see another boat for hours. Sometimes his sisters would go with us when they came up, or Ty would bring friends. Most of the time it was just the three of us, and we had a great time. We called ourselves "the Three Musketeers." We often took the boat to Lake Tahoe, and Ty would have friends hanging out on the beach somewhere. We'd pick them up in our boat for the day and hang out together.

Marc was a great father to Ty, and they were the best of friends. They thoroughly enjoyed each other's company and could talk for hours about anything from school to politics to scientific mysteries. Often I would read and let them be.

Ty had moved in and out of the house several times over the years, living with roommates from time to time, and then he'd come back home. He would work during the day and play music in the evenings. We so looked forward to his next performance.

One day he asked his sister Chanti if he could take her dog Scooby home with him. Scooby was a boxer. Ty had previously lived with his girlfriend, who had a dog that he had gotten very attached to. When they broke up, he missed the dog so much that Chanti agreed to let Ty have Scooby on a trial basis. He had more time to spend with Scooby than she did, since she was a single mom at that time and had a second big dog at home.

Ty was excited to have a dog again, and it opened up a new world to Scooby. Scooby went everywhere with him. He rode in Ty's truck, went to band practice, swam at Lake Tahoe, and went to the local bars that were dog friendly. He went along for the ride just about anywhere Ty went. This was an exciting time for Ty as he had a new buddy. Scooby had a friend named Elvis who lived at the house with him also. Elvis was some sort of English bulldog. They got along well, and everything was great for a couple of months.

One evening in October 2006, during band practice at the house, someone had left the front door open, and Scooby got out of the house. He ran down the street, as a skateboarder caught his eye. Ty chased after Scooby. When he grabbed the dog by the back of the neck, the dog turned around and repeatedly bit his right arm. Scooby was scared and would not let go of Ty's arm. I think possibly it hurt Scooby when Ty grabbed him by the back of his neck, so he turned around and bit Ty, but he would not let go. Ty picked Scooby up, ran home, and threw him in the backyard. Later, Ty reflected on this freak accident, believing the dog reacted unexpectedly because a roommate, who was jealous of him and showed hatred toward Scooby, mistreated the dog.

Ty was bloody and did not know what to do. He called me to let me know what was going on. He had no health insurance. I asked if he needed to go to the emergency room. He said he would wait until the morning, as it was late and he was tired, and he would clean his wounds up the best he could for now. A roommate's girlfriend was a nurse in training and helped clean him up.

I tried not to think about this, but I was very upset. With Ty, there was always craziness going on. He was always getting hurt and having to go to the hospital for something, so it didn't totally freak me out, but I was worried and had a difficult time falling asleep that night. I had no idea how serious the dog bite was.

The next day I was at work and went outside to take a walk on my morning break. I was talking to my boss when Ty walked up to us in a panic. He had been working across the street from me at a law office, and he came over to show me his arm, streaked with red lines and several puncture wounds. We both took one look at him and said he needed to go to the hospital.

Ty went to the emergency room and they admitted him into the hospital immediately. His arm was badly discolored and infected. Had he waited a few more hours, he would have lost his arm and possibly his life. Ty remained in the hospital for five days on IVs. He could not take it in there any longer, knowing the bills were mounting, and he left the hospital. The hospital did not want him to leave at that time, but agreed to let him go home on an IV with a nurse visiting to check on his progress for the next six weeks. During this recovery, many of Ty's friends thought he had fallen off the face of the earth. Some even told stories, and rumors developed about drug abuse. Meanwhile, these people did not care enough to check on him; only a few very close friends inquired.

After a long recuperation, Ty ended up moving back home with Marc and me. Ty was never the same after the dog bite.

PART II

Problems Mount— Something is Wrong

Ty soon started having all kinds of physical problems. Ty was not well, but in the beginning, he hid his illness from Marc and me for the most part. We knew he had some good and bad days, but we did not know how sick he really was. Every time he got ill, he had to go to the emergency room because he had no insurance; it was crazy. Nobody knew what was wrong with him, and the emergency room gave Ty medicine and sent him on his way. Ty looked forward to being in his job long enough to obtain insurance and get help from a doctor. It was six months before he could sign up for insurance through his work.

Ty got better, or so it seemed, and he was back at work for a couple of months. He called me one day and asked if I could meet him when I took my afternoon break. He worked across the street from me at a large law office, and we often took breaks with each other. I took one look at him, and he burst into tears. I thought, Oh my God, what is wrong? He said his boss had fired him. This was the day before he was to receive his health benefits. Ty was distraught because he had hoped to finally find out what was causing all the pain he was experiencing. Until that day, neither Marc nor I knew how sick he was and how important it was to him to get his health insurance. Ty wanted to find a doctor who could help him. He was devastated. The emergency room would just give Ty drugs and send him home. They did not know what was wrong with him. He had been hiding his medical issues from both of us and all his friends until his pain had gotten so bad he could no longer do so. When his pain would get unbearable, he would go straight to the emergency room and not tell anyone. Around this same time, he called his sister one day, sharing that he believed he had cancer.

Ty's physical problems got worse. He had extensive inflammation throughout his whole body, arthritic-type symptoms, and vasculitis; pain moved to various areas of his body. There were days when he physically could not get out of bed or even walk. His feet and ankles swelled so badly that he could not put on a pair of shoes. At times, he developed ulcers in his mouth, making it difficult to eat or swallow. He also developed ulcers on his nose, which at times bled. This left significant scarring. Embarrassed, he sometimes left the house with a bandage over his nose to cover his scarring. Family members suggested that Ty must be doing drugs, which caused the ulcers on his nose. Worst of all, however, ulcers on his genitals bled for more than seven months straight. I later found out that when he was working, he sometimes wore a condom all day long so he would not bleed onto his clothes. He would go all day without urinating because he had to wear a condom. He had ulcer-type blisters between his toes, and they sometimes appeared between his fingers. His fingers cracked so severely they bled and swelled, making it unbearable for him to play his guitar. Each day his symptoms were different, and we kept a log of his symptoms. We never knew what to expect or how he would feel the next day. Ty even lost the vision in his left eye for a time.

At different times, he developed skin rashes and lesions on various parts of his body. They healed and then reappeared somewhere else on his body. These lasted for several weeks or months and then reappeared. There were days his pain was intolerable, but he looked forward to the good days, which may have been two good days throughout the whole month for him. It came to the point where we knew Ty could no longer work, and he was becoming more and more a recluse. He'd stay home, as he did not feel well, and he did not want to have to explain to his friends that he was sick.

During one of Ty's visits to the emergency room, an attending physician thought that Ty might have an autoimmune disorder called pemphigus vulgaris, which causes blisters on skin. This is a very rare disorder that effects one in one million people, and we were told that it is potentially life threatening. People of Jewish descent are more susceptible, developing it at an approximate age of sixty. Because Ty wasn't Jewish and was young, we felt hopeful that he did not have this horrible disease. Later, we were thankful that this rare, life-threatening autoimmune disease was ruled out.

I was desperate and wrote a letter to Dr. Phil who has a television show. We were at a loss and did not have a lot of money to spend. This was in July 2008. Through his television show, he has helped many people with physical problems or with mental or drug-related issues. I thought for sure he would contact us and invite us to his show to discuss Ty's illness, and maybe we could get some help for him. We never heard anything from Dr. Phil. What a disappointment that was. Once again, I felt my son had been failed and was up against another roadblock.

Ty applied for Social Security Disability but was told it would take a couple of years before he would receive any benefits. Ty had nothing but time, or so we thought. Then he could get Medicaid, and maybe somebody could diagnose him and help him with his pain instead of just masking his pain with the drugs he received from doctors who did not know what was wrong with him to begin with.

The three of us made the best of it and became very close. We did everything together. I had a calendar just for Ty's appointments with his doctors, and there were plenty of them. Luckily, I was in a position at work that allowed me to arrange my schedule to take Ty to all these medical appointments and still work. I was so very thankful for their understanding of what I was going through with Ty and letting me arrange my schedule so I could take Ty to his appointments. At the beginning of each week, Ty and I would go through the appointment book together and figure out what we had to do and where he and

I had to be at any given time. This was a difficult time for all of us, but we were determined to fight whatever it was that was attacking my son.

We bought Ty a bicycle, and he rode it on days when he felt good. This helped me to take off work less often, but it was short-lived. Ty's illness affected his brain, causing him to have poor balance and become disoriented and forgetful. He started falling off his bicycle quite often when out riding, and at one point, a car almost ran over him. I encouraged him to not ride his bicycle on the busy streets.

Ty's love of music kept him busy and took his mind off his pain. He continued to write and play when he felt well and his fingers were not bleeding or swollen.

Ty did not get out of the house much, as he was in constant pain. He was confined to the house. He received some help from a clinic in Reno, but in order to get help from this clinic, he had to also go to the Northern Nevada Adult Mental Health Center. They could only prescribe medicine for him. Unfortunately, they overprescribed pain medication for him. At one point, Ty became so lethargic he was walking around drooling like a baby. He was shuffling his feet and could hardly walk. It was so heartbreaking to watch my son go downhill like this. I thought, What are you doing to my son? I was afraid for him and afraid I would lose him.

There was just so much Ty's doctor at Adult Services could do for him, as he had no idea what was wrong with him. I believe he really cared for Ty, but his hands were tied, as Ty had no insurance and was at their mercy. They could only give him medication for his pain. The medication helped some, but it only masked his problems, and he was not getting any better. We still had a two-year wait for Medicaid!

Ty was very lonely at home all day by himself while Marc and I were at work. I made every effort to come home from work at lunch every day to check on him and have lunch with him to kind of break up his day. I enjoyed being with

Ty whenever I could, but I felt bad that he was alone so much of the time, so I tried to be there for him. Ty went over to the next-door neighbors' house and visited with them quite often. He was so lonely during this time and thoroughly enjoyed their company, as they did his.

During a visit to Chanti's over the Fourth of July 2008, Ty's symptoms were nearly unbearable. Aside from the typical inflammatory symptoms, he was drooling, could barely speak, and his short-term memory was affected. We took him to the UC Davis Medical Center at the advice of one of Chanti's friends, to see a doctor in the Sacramento area. After many tests and much debating, the lead doctor returned to the examination room and reported the findings. They believed Ty had a rare autoimmune disorder called Behcet's disease, which is genetic in origin, but comes about following a traumatic event to the body. The doctors directed Ty to seek confirmation of the diagnosis by a professional, experienced in this disorder.

Chanti found the main doctor in this area of study in the United States located at New York University Medical Center.

Chanti first called this doctor about her brother and explained his symptoms and physical problems. After several contacts through e-mails and telephone conversations, it was agreed that Ty and Chanti would go to New York City to meet with this doctor. They were on a plane within a few weeks. All Ty's medical records were sent to the doctor in advance so he could review Ty's records before they met.

I remember this being such an exciting time for all of us, as we believed Ty was finally going to get well. We were going to get him the help he needed, and Ty would feel good again. We all felt so positive about this visit to New York City!

In August 2008, they met with the doctor in New York City. Chanti told me how hard it was for Ty on that day. He had a high level of pain throughout his body, and they had to walk all over New York City. His legs hurt horribly and were so very swollen. The extensive inflammation affected his entire body. At one point that day, he had to stop walking, as his legs hurt so badly. He just laid against a large rock in the park to rest his body until he could continue any farther. It had been months since Ty was able to wear a closed-in shoe, as his feet and ankles were so swollen.

Within an hour, the great doctor confirmed the diagnosis, describing how his presentation was classic. Ty had a high amount of inflammation throughout his body; the vasculitis; mouth sores, genital sores, cracking on his feet and hands that at times would bleed. We were told that Behcet's can also cause blindness. Ty later lost the vision in his left eye, but after treatment, his eyesight returned. Now that a doctor had diagnosed him, we were optimistic and believed he would get better.

Following this trip, and armed with direction for treatment from a highly regarded doctor, there was hope. This was soon shattered, when doctors in Reno, Nevada, failed to take advice from the expert, stating that we had just bought a diagnosis. The great doctor in New York could not prescribe medication across state borders, so Ty was stuck.

The doctors in Reno would not communicate with the doctor in New York. The Reno doctors did not know anything about this autoimmune disease, as it was so rare, and they did not know how to treat Ty. We now had a diagnosis but were once again hit with a roadblock. We were disappointed repeatedly, but we never lost hope that Ty would get well again.

The doctor in New York City had told Chanti and Ty during their visit that though one can die from Behcet's, most people do not die from the disease itself. Behcet's is like an umbrella with many related problems that make it difficult to fight off illnesses. The chances are greater that one will die from an illness other than Behcet's because of the weakened immune system.

During this time, the inflammation in his body was so high that he was swollen all over, including his face. His legs felt tight, and his looks even changed because of the swelling. This embarrassed him. He had received high dosages of steroids for his inflammation, causing weight gain. As a body builder, it was difficult for him to watch this transition taking place within himself. I tried reassuring him that this was all temporary and that he would feel good again one day.

At one point, it got to where Ty could not drive any longer. He awoke one morning and found that he had lost one-third of his peripheral vision in his left eye. Our eye doctor referred Ty to the only neuro-ophthalmologist in Nevada. He was highly specialized in his field. Because of this doctor's specialty, Adult Services would not pay for Ty to go see him. Marc and I did not care at this point; we wanted Ty to be able to see out of his left eye again, so we paid, and I took him to see this doctor. We just wanted our son well again. This was just another obstacle, but we would get through it together.

Once again, we had great hopes that Ty would get better. When I took Ty to see this doctor, and when he found out that Ty had Behcet's, he was so excited to meet Ty and try to help him. The doctor knew all about Behcet's, so he was excited about his new patient. He put Ty on a high dosage of steroids for his inflammation. Ty hated being on the steroids, but we hoped this was to be temporary. He also said that Ty would need to get infusions, which would help with the loss of his sight in his one eye. We needed to get a referral from Ty's doctor, so he could get these infusions through the cancer clinic in Reno.

When Ty and I went back to his Adult Services doctor, we told him what had transpired at the neuro-ophthalmologist's office. This doctor put in a request for Ty to go to the cancer clinic in Reno so that he could get the infusions he needed. It took some time, but his referral finally came through. We were so thankful.

I took Ty to the cancer clinic for three consecutive days. Ty received infusions twice a day for each of those three days, four hours each time. I sat with Ty at each of those appointments. Ty was very upbeat and positive throughout this ordeal. People we were sitting with were a lot worse off than Ty, and I think he felt very fortunate to be alive and have me there with him for moral support. Some of these people were very much alone, and it was a sad sight to see. Ty tried to cheer them up and make conversation with some of them.

I remember it was snowing during this time. While riding to his appointments, Ty had to wear sunglasses, as the snow was so bright that it would hurt his eyes. Even after the snow had melted away, there was that white-line divider in the roadways that hurt his eyes. It was pretty sad. Times were grim during this time, not knowing whether his vision would come back. It was hard for Ty not to be depressed. During this time, Ty started to teach himself how to play the piano. He was so afraid that he would become totally blind one day, and he wanted to have another outlet for himself during his dark hours. He would sit at the piano for hours, and it came easily for him. I felt his pain and wished I could take it away from him.

After some time, Ty got his vision back in his left eye. He was so thankful for that. Once Ty's eyesight returned following the infusions, the specialist he had seen for his eye was no longer interested in Ty as a patient.

Ty and I had many conversations, and I told him each time he was being referred to a new doctor, that soon he would be out of pain; we just had to wait for his next appointment. This gave us both hope. Then, we'd go to the appointment, and we'd both be so disappointed that nothing had changed. His pain would still be there, and the doctors would give him more drugs. I felt so helpless, as there was nothing I could do but be there for him. I remember on one occasion, Ty and I waited at this clinic to see a specialist who only came in once a month to this office. We waited in a room for two hours for the doctor to see Ty, and the doctor left the office without seeing him. They had forgotten we were even there because we had been there so long. We were both so disappointed and angry. We discussed suicide, and I begged him to please never do that. Had he done so, I could not have blamed him one bit, as I felt his pain right along with him.

All but a few of Ty's friends at this time kind of disappeared and wanted nothing to do with him. They did not understand his illness and felt he just wanted the pain meds that the doctors were giving him. Ty became extremely lonely; his symptoms kept getting worse, with no end in sight. He was very depressed.

Ty was alone much of the time. He had a girlfriend, but she could not be with him all the time, as she worked. He had lots of time on his hands and needed companionship. There was only so much Marc and I could do for Ty. We both had to work and could not be with him all the time, either. He decided he wanted to get a puppy, so the three of us went to the animal shelter, and Ty found a puppy. As it turned out, someone who volunteered at the shelter took the puppy Ty wanted, and Ty left without a puppy that day. He was devastated and angry at the same time as to what transpired. We went home that day, and Ty searched on the Internet. After some time, he found a puppy in Yuba City. The next day, a Sunday in January, Marc and Ty made the two-hour drive to see the puppy.

Later that day they brought home a puppy about six weeks old that Ty named Yuba. This was a crazy-looking puppy, tiger striped with large ears, very colorful with a colorful personality! Yuba weighed about eight pounds.

A week had passed and we noticed one morning that Yuba became lifeless and we had no idea what was wrong with the little guy. We took Yuba to the veterinarian, who told us that he had parvo. Yuba's chances for survival were slim. He was so sick he looked like he was going to die. The veterinary hospital was going to charge an astronomical amount of money to have Yuba hospitalized, and we did not have the money. Ty asked them what he needed to do to save his puppy.

Ty gave Yuba IV solutions to keep him alive and after a few days, Yuba started to perk up and was fine. He saved his puppy. This was a real bonding time for Ty and Yuba. After this, Yuba slept with Ty and was always with him. They became the best of buddies.

Yuba fit in with our family quite well and took on many of Ty's traits. Ty was in pain a lot of the time and at night was awake with Yuba next to him, and then he would sleep during the day, as he was so exhausted from being up all night. Yuba was always by his side.

Around this time, Ty met some new friends and was writing music and playing guitar. He had a girlfriend, Sarah, who was here a lot, and we liked her very much. She and Ty were good for each other. During that time, they needed each other as well; it worked for them.

Ty seemed to be very content at this time in his life. Though he could not work, he was feeling better about himself and not so depressed. He battled with his pain every day, but he was resigned to the fact that his life had changed and would never be the same. He had a girlfriend, his dog, a family who loved him, and he was writing and playing music. Marc and I were resigned to the fact that Ty would most probably live with us forever—and maybe his girlfriend too. We were OK with that.

Nevertheless, Ty's pain was horrible. He was taking a load of pain medication, which was not helping all that much, and neither we nor the doctors in Reno knew what to do for him.

Ty was so desperate to get health insurance so he could get better services for himself. He and I went together to talk to the Department of Welfare and Supportive Services about receiving assistance. We were told he was not eligible. The supervisor at that location came out and told us that if Ty were to have a child or a pregnant girlfriend who lives with him, that the office would give him health benefits. I was furious by this and told her, "You have got to be kidding! My son cannot take care of himself now, and you are saying to go have a baby? There is definitely something wrong with this picture!"

§

Before Ty told Marc and me he was sick, he had gotten involved with illegal drugs. Keep in mind, this was a year after rumors flew about when he was home hooked up to an IV. Nobody believed there was anything wrong with him, and the doctors had no idea what was wrong; he felt alienated by everyone and became desperate enough that he chose to do drugs. He had told us that because he did not have medical insurance he would go straight to the emergency room when the pain was unbearable. He had accumulated over $200,000 in medical bills. It seemed no amount of pain medications helped the pain, so he took to the street and bought drugs there for his pain. Nobody knew what he was going through. He was in horrible shape at one point and not living with us then, so we did not notice. We knew something was up but did not know he was sick. He felt nobody could help him and he became desperate and very much alone.

Evidently, his friends did not know he was sick either, and they just thought Ty enjoyed doing drugs. Ty did not tell anyone how sick he was. He did not want people feeling sorry for him. His longtime girlfriend did not have a clue he was ill and said she would never have left him had she known. This was why he kept it to himself; he had his pride and did not want people feeling sorry for him.

Ty continued having to take large amounts of pain medication for his pain on a daily basis. Our house looked like a pharmacy! At least now, the drugs he was taking were legal, and a doctor prescribed them. His pain would move to different parts of his body. It was never the same two days in a row. Some days he felt like he had a bad case of the flu. His body ached all over, and he felt weak and fatigued. He slept a lot when he could but it was difficult because of the pain, and it would keep him awake throughout the night. At times, he had difficulty with his memory and concentration. He also got dizzy, and his balance was affected. Occasionally, he would get migraine headaches.

During this time, many of Ty's friends did not believe he was sick and dissociated themselves from him. For the most part, our family did not believe Ty was sick either, until he was finally diagnosed with Behcet's syndrome. Even then, many looked the other way. It was a lonely time for him, but he was doing pretty well, considering he really did not have much of a life besides Mom and Dad, his girlfriend, Sarah, and his faithful dog, Yuba.

Ty moved back home with us after we realized that he was not doing drugs recreationally. There were rules he had to abide by. He could take only medications prescribed by his doctor at Adult Services and by doctors at the Northern Nevada Adult Services. I monitored all his medications from then on, and we told him he could no longer live in our house if he were to do any illegal drugs. It was difficult because the pain was so horrible for him, and his pain medications just dulled his pain. He tried everything during this time: soaking in warm baths, meditation, playing guitar—anything to take his mind away from what he was feeling inside his body.

It is hard for people on the outside to understand that someone can be so sick while looking well. He didn't always look so well, though. We heard this so many times from family, friends, and his doctors. Nobody knew what was going on in Ty's body but Ty. Nobody knew about Behcet's and how to treat it. Doctors gave Ty drugs for the pain and steroids for the inflammation in his body. Marc and I were with him every day and saw what he was going through. We felt so helpless; we could do nothing to make it better for him. Why wouldn't he get better? Why wouldn't his pain go away? The pain medication was just masking his problems but not curing them. I just wanted to take his pain away from him. It broke my heart to see my son in such pain.

Ty was a sensitive and caring person. I received a call at work from Ty one day that there was a fire across the street from our house, and it was headed up the canyon. He told me that our neighborhood most probably would need to be evacuated. At the time, Marc was working in Carson City, a good forty-five minutes away from our home. I was worried about our dog at the time, Gunner. I told Ty to bring Gunner to my work, and I would take care of him there. Ty brought Gunner and important files to me for safekeeping. Then he headed back home. The fire was getting out of hand and very close to the houses nearby, and the police were not letting people into the area. Ty noticed a school bus full of children and had to stop the driver from dropping off the children at the bus stop at the end of our street. The school bus driver was so distressed that he did not know what to do in this emergency situation, but Ty took charge and told him under no circumstances could these kids be dropped off in the middle of a fire! The bus driver listened to Ty and drove the kids to safety. Ty also helped our immediate neighbors with getting their belongings from their homes to their vehicles and helping them to their safety, as everyone was told to evacuate the area because the fire was very close. After several hours, we were all allowed to return to our homes, and we were so very thankful that the fire department saved our neighbors and our homes.

February 9, 2009, was our twenty-fourth wedding anniversary. As usual, Marc and I went to work that day and Ty was at home. He did not have any money to buy us an anniversary card, but being the kind of person he was, he started drawing. He drew us a picture of flowers for our anniversary. He spent five hours doing this for us, and it is one of the most treasured gifts he ever gave us. We framed the picture, and it hangs on our living room wall as a reminder to us of a much happier time. Ty also left me little notes that were so sweet and kind.

Ty loved going to college, and at one point had to quit school because he had no money, and he was ill. My younger, brother, Jon, and his wife, Melinda, came to Ty one day and asked him if he would like to go back to school. Of course, Ty was all over that. He was so excited. They told him if he were to take one course at a time, and he received an A for that course, that they would reimburse him for that class. Ty could then register to take another course and do the same. Ty was excited by this opportunity, and he immediately enrolled at the University of Reno. He finally had something to look forward to in his life. This was the start of a new beginning, or so he thought.

Ty was very excited about going back to school. This would keep his mind off his illness, and he would be around people his age. His illness had kept him home most of the time, and he was very lonely. He found out that the class he had enrolled in had about a mile-long walk from where he had to park a vehicle and get to the class. The vasculitis in his legs was often so horrible that sometimes he could barely walk. His feet and ankles swelled horribly that he told me he could not walk that distance. Ty made an appointment with a rheumatologist he had seen in Reno many times. He hoped the doctor would write a letter on his behalf that he could take to the Department of Motor Vehicles so that he could apply for a handicap placard.

Once again, Ty was hit with a roadblock! This doctor refused to give him a letter and told Ty, "I know you are in pain, but you look healthy. People on campus will try to pick a fight with you for parking in a handicap lot when you look good." I will never forget this, and we never went back to see this doctor again.

We were both so disappointed and angry at the same time over this. I told Ty that we would somehow get him to class. "You look good." Ty had heard this so many times from doctors and friends. Nobody knew the pain that was going on inside his body other than Marc and me, as we lived with it daily and saw what Ty was going through. I believe his sisters understood this also, as they were very close to Ty.

It is unfortunate Ty passed away before he ever got to start his class at the university. When I called the office of the doctor who would not write the letter for Ty to let them know he had passed away, they were extremely curt and cold to me. They probably were in shock that a twenty-nine-year-old would die so suddenly. It had only been about six weeks since he had seen the doctor and was denied his help. I think a lot of people may think you are physically well because you look like you are healthy on the outside, when they have no idea what is going on with you on the inside. Many times, Ty did not look good on the outside, either, as his face was so bloated from the extensive inflammation he had in his body and the drugs his doctor placed him on for his pain. I do not believe many people thought Ty was sick, and Ty was not one to complain to others about his pain. He just retreated within himself—a world that had changed so dramatically for him, and he had come to accept.

In September 2009, both Marc and Ty were working on our roof. They were trying to replace some rock that had fallen off the chimney.

I received a telephone call from Ty just before noon while I was at work. He told me that the ladder collapsed underneath Marc as he was coming down from the roof, and he fell flat on his back against the benches on the deck, rolled down the wooden stairs, and landed on the cement. Marc was unconscious and laid there until the fire department and ambulance arrived. I left work immediately and was home in minutes. We later found out that Marc had broken his back. He was in intensive care for five days and does not remember that time being in the hospital. Both Ty and I were with Marc almost around the clock during this time. Marc and Ty were always close but became even closer during this time, as now they were both home together all day long while I went to work.

The swine flu made news in 2009. It was a horrible flu with people sick everywhere. It was a scary time because people were afraid they would get this horrible flu. Ty had to be very careful not to be around anyone sick because of his Behcet's and his compromised immune system. One of the medications he received was a cancer-type medication that caused his white blood count to be very low and made it difficult for him to fight off illnesses. I just remember his being so tired, as he would be up all night awake in pain and he'd be so exhausted during the day, so he would nap often. His dog, Yuba, was always by his side.

One evening he did not feel particularly well, and a friend of his had called and asked him to go out and watch a local band play some music. Ty said he just wanted to be home, that he was not feeling so well, and he was tired. I remember Ty telling me his friend was upset with him at the time because he did not feel like going out that evening.

Then Ty told me he did not have long to live. He was twenty-nine at the time, and I said, "Why do you say that, Ty?"

He said, "I just know."

I just looked at him very sadly and said, "Don't say that."

Ty was on the floor with Yuba. He had rested his head on the couch and fallen asleep.

I will never forget this evening. Previous to this conversation, Ty had told me when he leaves this place that he wants to be cremated, and he told me exactly what he wanted me to do with his ashes. I thought it was very interesting at the time that he would be bringing up such a topic to me, though we had conversations about everything. Sometimes Ty would tell me things I did not want to hear about himself or others. He told me, "Please do not put me in the ground. It takes up too much land. Besides, we are energy when we pass on, and it's crazy to spend all that money, as I won't be in some expensive box underground." He was adamant that I get this right. I did not think too much about this conversation after that evening.

Two weeks later, I heard Ty up in the night. This was very normal for him, as he could not sleep being in pain, and most nights, he was up. I also noticed that the toilet was being flushed quite often, and that was what woke me up, the sound of running water.

One of the medicines he took was a cancer-type medicine, which treated him for pain but also had horrible side effects. It made him vomit almost on a daily basis. I wanted to get up to see how he was doing, but I felt maybe I would be bothering him, as I thought his girlfriend was at the house, so I never got up to see how he was. He stayed awake in pain with Yuba by his side almost every night, as his pain was unbearable. Then Yuba and he would sleep most of the day. Yuba took on Ty's traits and was almost humanlike. We used to call Yuba Ty's younger brother. After some time, I fell back to sleep.

The next morning, I woke up early as usual and started to get ready for work. It was October 12, 2009. This day I will never forget. Ty came out of his bedroom and we talked like most mornings. Ty was following me around the house talking with me as I was getting ready for work. At one point I remember he made himself some homemade soup. He was so excited about making this tomato bisque soup. He loved to cook and as he was not feeling well, having been up the night before, and he thought maybe the soup would make him feel better. Ty would watch the cooking channel during the day while at home and make these incredible meals later for us.

I told Ty I had heard him up in the night, but I did not want to bother him because I thought his girlfriend, Sarah, was with him. I also wondered if he might have the swine flu, because of his increased vomiting. The drugs he was on made him vomit, but not to this degree. I just felt something was not right. I asked Ty if he needed me to be there for him that day, and he said no, that he would be all right. He was sure that his soup was going to make him feel better. Ty asked me if I would be coming home from work that day at lunch, and I told him yes. I left Ty that morning at about 6:40 a.m. to go to work. He had fallen asleep on the couch after he had eaten his soup. I kissed him good-bye and left for work. Marc was asleep in the back bedroom, recuperating from his back injury.

Sarah, Ty's girlfriend found him that awful day in October, lying in his bed with his dog, Yuba, beside him. Evidently, after I left for work, Ty had awakened and brought Yuba to bed with him and had closed his door to not disturb Marc. When Sarah got to the house that morning, she went to Ty's room and knew something was not right. She felt Ty and he was cold to the touch, so she ran to the back bedroom for Marc's help. They could not revive him. If only I had not gone to work that day and had spent a few more moments with my son...

I received a call at noon from Marc that Ty was not breathing and to get home now. I had been covering the lunch hour phones that day and had answered the phone when Marc called. I remember I got up and just said to everyone who was in the room, "My son's not breathing. I'm going home." I worked about three miles from home, and I think I probably made it home in two minutes.

Crazy things ran through my head, as I raced home to find my son on the living room floor on his back, lying very peacefully. It never crossed my mind that he would be dead when I walked through the front door. I will never forget it as long as I live. When I stood there looking at Ty, I could tell that his soul had already left his body. I don't know how to explain this, but I just knew by looking at Ty, and I said to myself, he is finally out of pain and in peace. I am sure I must have been in shock because I just stood there looking at him. He looked so peaceful, as if he were sleeping. I could not even cry because I knew his pain was now gone and he was in a better place. He tried to tell me he was leaving two weeks ago, but I had no idea it would be this soon.

Family was called and came up from California to be with Marc and me for the next week. It kept our attention elsewhere. I didn't know how or where to begin to plan a funeral for my son. This would be so final, and I could not bear it. I couldn't think straight and just did not want to think about it at all. All my thoughts were on Ty day and night. I could think of nothing else. During this time, both our daughters were like our angels. They did everything for us and helped us through this horrible time, though they were grieving just the same for their brother. I remember not being able to sleep well or eat. I felt guilty for doing either of these things that we all take for granted in our daily lives. How was I to go on without my son? I wasn't sure I wanted to go on living. I knew this was a selfish thought, as I had other children I love and care about deeply, but I was so distraught, and Ty was all I could think about.

About a week later we had a memorial for Ty at the Chism House in Reno. This is an old Reno home with a gigantic yard and garden area, with a large pond with ducks. The surrounding area is very pretty and serene with beautiful flowers and colorful plants. The time of year was autumn, so the colors of the garden were breathtaking, and the trees were turning orange, yellow, and red. This particular day started out cloudy, and we later had some sun filtering through the white puffy clouds. Later in the day the clouds turned dark, as though the heavens were angry at the time. Many weddings are held at this location. With our daughter's help and Ty's friends, this day could not have been more special for Ty. It was unbelievable. I am sure he was looking down at his sisters proudly. I was told by a friend I hadn't met yet, Marti, that Ty's memorial was so big it should have been held at Lawlor Events Center. She was right. It was a pleasant day, and I believe every friend Ty ever knew came. Every band he played in from years past attended, several of his friends played guitar and organ, and some sang. Some of our friends even danced. I am sure Ty was loving this.

I had written a memorial letter to my son, but I did not think I would be able to read it. I asked Tammi, a very good friend of Ty's, if she could do that for me, and she said she would be happy to. When it came time to read my letter, I got the courage to read it myself, and I was so glad I did. I have never been able to speak in front of so many people before, but I believe Ty helped me on this day. I would have done anything for him. My two daughters pulled together a beautiful slide show with pictures of Ty and the family from when he was a baby until his death. The slide show was synchronized with music. It was a beautiful day, though sad, as our lives would never be the same without our son. One of Ty's dearest friends said the clouds hovered over the crowd like angels' wings that day.

Everyone handles death differently, and I never really knew how I felt about death until Ty's passing. I wanted to know where the hell he went. What happens when you die? I started to read anything I could about death and passing. I needed to know anything I could on this subject. I felt great comfort in reading and still do. Books became my best friend.

I had gone to my doctor, who also had been Ty's doctor. I told her I was not sleeping and was very depressed. She asked me if I was religious or maybe spiritual. I told her I was not religious; I considered myself to be spiritual, if anything. I had not thought about it much. She then suggested that I see a psychologist, and she said medication for relaxation might help me sleep. I was hardly sleeping during this time and would lie awake at night feeling guilty that I was alive, and my son was not here with us.

I took my doctor's advice and made an appointment with a psychologist. I went to a psychologist for a short period, and I liked her very much. She had me try some medication that would take the edge off things and hopefully help me to sleep. I did not like the way it made me feel, so I stopped the medication almost immediately after starting it.

I continued to see this psychologist, but it felt like we were friends rather than doctor and patient. There were times when I would go see her that I felt she was going to cry for me, and I was consoling her. She had young children, and I think she was trying to put herself in my shoes. She felt sad when thinking it could have been her who had lost a child. Nevertheless, I continued to go back to see her for a few more times, as I thought maybe I needed to do this; besides, I liked her. After a few months, I decided that I did not need her services, that she was more like a friend to me, so I moved on. I continued to read book after book, trying to find the answers I needed so badly. Where did my son go?

It had been two weeks after Ty's passing that I went back to work. I could have taken more time for myself and stayed home from work, but I needed to keep busy and not sit at home feeling sorry for myself. I think at that time I needed to get my life back to some sort of routine and normalcy, if that was at all possible. I didn't know what I felt exactly or how I was supposed to act or feel after losing someone I loved so greatly.

When I went back to work, it felt strange to be there. I did not feel comfortable, and I felt great loneliness, though there were people all around me. I went through the motions, and I think I was numb during this time. I think I needed to be at work to keep busy and not think about what I was going through and my grief. I held my emotions in. As soon as I left for lunch and got into my vehicle to go home at lunchtime, I would let go and cry my eyes out! So many days I came back to work after lunch having broken down, and I felt embarrassed coming back to work because my eyes were so red and puffy. All I wanted was to be at home where I felt safe and could cry if I wanted, let go, and not have to explain to anyone the pain I was going through.

When you lose someone, it is as if nobody knows what to say to you, so they ignore you like you have some sort of disease or something they will catch if they speak to you. I continued reading my books on death and the afterlife, and occasionally someone at work would ask what I was reading. When I would tell them, they would look at me as if I was a freak.

I did not expect long conversations when people are so uncomfortable with the subject of death, but a hello or good morning would have made me feel better and not like I was such an outcast. I had worked with these people for almost ten years at the time, and they could not say hello—geez. I felt very much alone and sad, so I kept to myself most of the time. I was not angry; I just felt like I did not belong there and needed to be somewhere else where I could grieve and just be me.

There were days when I would not want to talk, and I would definitely keep to myself for the most part. It was difficult, and if I'd had a particularly bad day and started to cry, someone would come up and ask, "What is wrong?" Like, oh sure, I am supposed to get over the death of my son in a month? Let me tell you, you never get over it. It is something you learn to accept. You have to go on the best you can, but you never get over it.

PART III
One Mother's Loss and Learning to Live Again

I WAS IN THE BATHROOM getting ready for work one morning, and I heard a noise in the window above me. I looked up and saw a red-tailed hawk sitting on the windowsill. I found it interesting that this hawk had pushed itself up against the window. This was to be the beginning of my experiences with seeing many beautiful hawks that would appear around me at different locations and at my home. Hawks are messengers, and they appeared to come to me when I needed emotional support on days when I felt sad and needed to feel connected with my son. I could be walking Yuba and see a beautiful hawk that would fly directly above me as we walked, or I might be driving down the highway and have one fly over my car. They have appeared countless times in my backyard, circling above my house, or sitting in a tree in the backyard, and they appear to be looking at me. I know this sounds strange to most, but for me it is very comforting. When a hawk appears before me, I feel a very strong connection with Ty—as if he is giving me a sign that he is thinking of me.

The next day, Chanti and my grandson Isaac were visiting us. The next-door neighbors had their grandkids at the house, and they were all out in the front yard playing soccer. We all walked over with Yuba and joined in the fun. Yuba loved playing with the kids. I looked up into the sky, and I saw a red-tailed hawk circling above us as the kids played ball. The hawk stayed there for some time, as though he was watching over the kids. I could not help but think of my son and how he used to love to play with these kids! Ty was such a kid himself.

On my way to work I would find myself talking to Ty aloud inside the car and asking him to help me to be strong so that I could make it through my work-day. I loved my job, though it was very stressful at times. I prayed to Ty for me to be at peace, and I would tell him how much I loved him every chance I got. I started to notice little things happening around me, and I just knew it was Ty here with me in some strange way. I would try to listen to music, but it would make me sad, and I would cry. Suddenly the music would just stop playing. I feel my son was behind that. He did not want his mother to be sad.

During this time, Marc was working about an hour out of town. He had long visits with Ty on his way to and from work. They had been so very close. Marc found a place on top of a hill near work where he would go to feel Ty's presence. Wild horses appeared daily in this serene, quiet setting. At times, Marc could almost see Ty standing on top of the hill among the horses. Marc would go to this special place to talk to Ty and find comfort. He would come home in the evening and tell me of these special events.

Before Ty passed, he was learning to play John Lennon's song "I'm Only Sleeping" on the guitar. One morning before work, I listened to that song on my CD player at home. I cried my eyes out while listening to it. This song is one of my favorites by Lennon and it brings back so many memories of Ty playing it. He was so determined to teach himself how to play that song! I wanted to hear that song again and tried five times to go backward to play that song, and the CD player would not play it. This has happened to me on numerous occasions when I go to play something, and another song pops up in its place on the stereo. I think Ty controls my stereo! I began to notice that songs that were special to Ty and me would come on the radio both at work and at home, and it would make my day. Every day I looked forward to any sign from my son.

Sarah told me that when her mother passed a couple of years before Ty, she sought help through a psychic medium. She gave me the medium's name, Marti Tote. Sarah thought this might help me get through this horrible time. Sarah had a very difficult time after Ty's passing. She could not even come back to our house after Ty left us; it was too hard. I think she just had to move on and follow her own path. They had loved each other very much, and it was just too much for her.

I thought going to a medium would be very interesting but very scary at the same time, as I had never gone to a medium or psychic before. I was definitely curious, and my curiosity took over. I had to know what happened to my son. So, he died, but where do you go when you die? I had no idea, and I needed to find answers.

On October 27, 2009, I was feeling horribly sad. Ty had only been gone a couple of weeks. I was listening to music on the radio, and Ty was seeing to it that I was hearing music I liked that helped me feel a connection to him. I believe he did not want me to feel sad.

Christmas was coming, and I was especially sad this year. I always loved Christmas, but this was going to be a difficult one for me, my first without my son. I went through the motions of decorating my desk as usual at work. I was trying to keep things as normal as possible, although I wasn't in the holiday spirit. I thought it might help me with my depression. A coworker gave me a tiny Santa mug as a decoration, and I placed it on top of the shelf above my desk along with my other ornaments. I loved Christmas decorations. I picked out a Christmas decoration, set Ty's picture in it, and placed it on our Christmas tree that year. Each year afterward, Marc and I have picked out an ornament for Ty and placed it on our Christmas tree in his memory.

This day was particularly hard day for me. It was December 1, 2009. I was on my way to work. I was asking for Ty's guidance. I felt as though he was my angel. I prayed to him and asked that he please help me get through this day. When I got to work, the first song that came on the radio was "Let's Stay Together," an Al Green song that Kristen, a friend of his, sang at his memorial service. Kristen did it spontaneously, and she made it so very special that day. Kristen had the most beautiful voice, and many people got up and danced. I just know Ty was there looking proudly down at all his friends. Ty always loved a party!

After listening to this song, I walked upstairs for a few minutes to do some filing. I walked back downstairs, and the first song on the radio was John Lennon's "I'm Only Sleeping." Ty knows how much I love this song and what a big Beatles fan I was since I was a kid, and we would listen to Beatles music quite often together. I believe Ty was sending me signs that I was going to be OK. My day ended up being a very pleasant day. I felt uplifted and fairly happy after receiving signs from my son. I felt guilty that maybe I was asking too much from him, but at the same time, I could not help myself. I needed him. It was the only way I could get on with my life here—having Ty in my life still.

Our first Christmastime without Ty was horrible. We would most often have Christmas Eve at home and then Christmas in California with Ty's sisters, and the rest of the family would come over with all the kids. It was hectic but loads of fun with kids running wild all over the place, opening packages. Ty was just like a kid himself and was great with them, so he was a big help. If anyone had a gift that needed assembly, Ty was right on it. Also, he was a terrific cook, along with Marc, so the two of them would head to the kitchen and cook dinner for everyone.

As time passes, I am finding myself becoming more spiritual. Maybe this is a gift that I always have had. I believe my son's passing has caused me to be more open to so many new things that I would never have imagined before he left us. I look for any signs my son sends to me. I miss him terribly—his beautiful smile, his contagious laugh, and his sense of humor. Even on the other side he has a sense of humor, unbelievable but true! I never would have thought I could have had a relationship with one who has passed, but Ty has shown me that it is possible; you just have to be open to it and not afraid. I am sure I know people out there who think I am nuts or maybe even obsessed with my son's passing. People should not be so quick to judge others; you never know what lies ahead for you and how you are going to feel when you lose someone so close to you. I myself did not know how I felt about death until Ty's passing. If someone said we would be communicating after his death, I would have thought the whole thing was crazy. Now I am living this, having lost him in the physical world, and yes, I am communicating with my son. Ty has shown me that this is possible. He has taught me so very much. I am grateful for what he has shown me and how I continue to learn and grow from him.

One Halloween, Ty was getting ready to go out, and he was dressing up along with his friends. They all had rented a limousine that night so they could cruise around to different establishments in town and drink. He asked if Marc and I would come to the house where he was living at the time and take pictures of everyone, as they were all dressed up. Ty had a female roommate at this time whose name was Tyler. I always thought it would be comical if they got together one day, but they were just friends. Tyler's friends all loved Ty. Ty came out from the other room, and he was dressed in a French maid costume with fishnet stockings! Oh my gosh! I about fell onto the floor laughing. I remember him showing me a pair of blue G-string underwear, and he said, "Geez, you guys wear these?" It was so hilarious. Needless to say, he did not put on the string bikini underwear! He and his friends went out that evening, and Ty wore the costume, but I guess he grew tired of it and changed. Ty was quite a character, and there was never a dull moment when he was around.

It got to where he looked forward to dressing up at Halloween. As a child, he never wanted to dress up for school when the kids could wear costumes the day of Halloween, and he never would.

I remember his band Steve Dave all dressing at Halloween as Mormons. They were to do a show that evening, and they all looked great all dressed so nicely in their beautiful suits. The boys always had such a good time together.

Another time Ty wore a bright, colorful country shirt, something that singer Garth Brooks would wear with tight jeans, along with cowboy boots. Ty was anything but country and did not like country music. He pulled it off though. He was a funny guy.

I believe my son will appear to me at times in the form of a hawk. Quite often a pair of hawks circled directly above our house. I believe they were Ty and my brother Gary. One day I was enjoying the sun on the deck in the backyard, and a hawk came down very low into the yard and looked as though he was going to land on my arm. That time it was a little close for comfort.

Yuba notices the hawks flying around our house also. I will say, "There is your daddy," and he looks straight up into the air at them. Marc and I can be walking Yuba down the street, and I hear the hawks flying above us. I never noticed this before Ty's passing. I can be driving down the freeway, talking to Ty or singing a song and hearing his voice in the background. When I look up, there will be a hawk above my car. I believe he watches out for me. When I travel, and especially when I'm alone, I feel his presence so strongly. I just know he is in the backseat! He always liked to go on a road trip with Marc and me.

I remember driving with Ty to see Chanti in California, and we were both singing the Shins' song "Saint Simon." I always called it the La La La song. We would sing it really loudly while driving down the highway, and now when I put that CD on in the car, I swear I hear Ty's voice singing that song right along with me. In years past, Ty, Chanti, my grandson Isaac, a friend, Marc, and I went to see the Shins at the Fox Theater in Oakland. This was the last concert we attended with Ty. He loved the Shins. It was a great evening and I took BART transportation for the first time.

Ty likes to play with electricity! When I wake up in the morning, I often notice a light on in another part of the house that had not been on before I went to bed the night before. He is not picky about which light he turns on. It is different all the time. Ty also likes to move my perfume bottles around on my dresser, and he moves change around that is sitting on my dresser. In Ty's bathroom—yes, I still call it Ty's bathroom—he has moved a glass from one end of the sink to the other.

Another trick Ty has learned since being on the "other side" is leaving different scents throughout the house. For instance, I might smell coffee brewing. I will go to the kitchen to see if Marc started a pot of coffee, and there is no coffee brewing! I smelled bubble gum one evening while sitting in my living room, and on other occasions, I smelled Ty's favorite cologne. I think Ty was trying to be funny one night, as my house smelled as though my dog pooped in it, something Yuba has never done, and there definitely was no poop anywhere. It was not my dog, and I could only guess that it was Ty playing games with us.

I believe Ty's dog, Yuba, sees him in our house and especially in Ty's bedroom. He will sometimes just lie in his bed and not leave Ty's bedroom. Outside, Yuba will be lying down on the deck, and out of the blue, he will get up and go crazy, running back and forth, making noises, and trying to jump up like he wants to be on the roof. I can say to Yuba, "Where are your angels?" and he runs outside and looks up at the roof in one particular area near the fireplace. I believe Ty is looking out over Yuba, and that he sees Ty on the roof. In the evening I feel Ty's presence when we are in the living room watching television. I know Ty is sitting right there watching it with us.

I have a favorite chair in the house, and many times, whether during the day or at night, while I'm reading, Ty will appear before me in the hallway, letting me know he is there, looking out after me.

Chanti gave me a wooden Halloween witch she purchased for me at a craft show. Every year, I place the witch in our hallway on top of our wooden CD cabinet. When Ty was alive, we had this little game we would play together. Ty liked the witch to face the front door, so when people walked up to the door they saw her. I liked to see her facing the other way, so when I sat on the sofa I could enjoy looking at her. So we would move her back and forth without saying a word to one another. This witch would prove to be significant later in Ty's story.

Three months after Ty passed, I was talking to him and asked him to show me a sign that I would know that he was still with me. I was on break from work and walking near Virginia Street in Reno, when my girlfriend, who was walking with me, said she heard a hawk. When we looked up, there happened to be two hawks, and they were circling directly above us. They were so beautiful. It was like they were soul mates dancing in the sky. They flew over the federal courthouse building then back over to us again, circled right above us again, and then flew over my work building at the time at One California Boulevard. I thanked Ty for the beautiful sign he gave me that day. These special signs always cheered me up and helped me get through another day. As my friend did not "believe," I did not explain what the hawks signified or what they meant to me. It did not matter, as I knew this to be a gift and a sign from Ty. I have become more receptive to receiving and acknowledging that these signs are for me and truly a gift.

After the holidays, I was packing up my Christmas stuff on my desk and surrounding work area when I came across the tiny Christmas Santa mug that a coworker gave me. I noticed inside were three pennies. They had not been there before. Nobody at work would have known what the three pennies meant to me. I feel this was my first Christmas gift from Ty from the other side. He was in the band Steve Dave for years, and they had written a song called "Four Pennies." It was about being on the road, and each penny stood for a member in the band, there being a total of four. At Ty's memorial, his bandmates sang this song and said, "But now there's only three pennies." I believe this was a gift from Ty to me.

A few days passed, and I don't know why, but on this particular date I decided to read chapters 7 and 8 in a Bible that a neighbor had left at my door. I don't know why I felt this need to pick it up and read it, and I wasn't sure what I even felt about the Bible, but I sure felt Ty's presence during this time. Shortly thereafter, as I was sitting in my living room reading, I glanced up and saw Ty looking through my large window just to the right of the front entryway. He was just watching me as I read this Bible. Ty was wearing a plain white T-shirt and tan shorts. He looked good. This was the first time Ty had come to visit me where I could actually see him as he had looked in the physical world. He did not say anything to me aloud. The two of us were silent, treasuring the moment, which seemed like minutes but lasted only seconds.

So what does all this mean? I had heard about after-death communications, "ADC," and this was to be the beginning of our communication. My father had visited me once but not like this. I was now beginning to notice more and more things happening around me. They would happen so often that there was no way these things could be coincidences. Ty had found his way to be present in my life even though he was no longer here in his physical self. To this day, it amazes me that he can do the things he does. When I think it is not possible that these things are happening, and that I must be imagining all this, Ty proves me wrong again and does something so fantastic that I no longer doubt myself. Then I know it is definitely Ty and this is real. I always believed Ty to be a very old soul, and he is a highly active spirit in the afterlife.

I was driving home one day at lunch to see Yuba. Ty was continuing to leave me signs on the radio. Ty was not placing songs on the radio that I wanted so badly to hear that reminded me of him; he would put a message inside my head, telling me to turn on the radio when one of our special songs was playing. I continued to feel sad, and I would tell him how much I missed him. At the same time, I would tell him that I knew he was in a better place now. But why can't you be here with me?

It was January 2010. I will never forget it. I looked over at the car next to me on my right, and the license plate said, "ALIVE." There was my sign, and from that point on, I started to notice many plates that had some sort of meaning to me or had just plain "TY" on them wherever I went. It was like he made sure I saw them. I would look at the driver and the plate, when somebody cut me off the road, and I would be angry, and notice it would happen to say "TY" something on it. Then my anger would go away. I figured Ty was just trying to get my attention and let me know he was thinking about me too. That's when I really started to read license plates! I had no idea how many had Ty's name on them until he passed away.

Two months after Ty's passing, I made an appointment with Marti. Making an appointment with a medium was the scariest thing I had ever done, but it was exciting at the same time for me.

MY FIRST VISIT WITH MARTI—MONDAY, FEBRUARY 1, 2010

When I first met Marti, she was not what I expected or could even envision, though I did not know what to expect from the get-go, as I had never been to a medium. She was a very attractive petite woman, warm and bubbly in nature, and pretty outspoken. I instantly liked her. She told me a little about herself and said the visit would be very relaxed. She would let the angels come to her. She could hear people from the other side when she turned to her right side. I was sitting across from her on a small loveseat-type couch, and she sat in a chair across from me. She told me that she would ask me yes-or-no questions, and we would go from there.

Marti's pleasantly decorated room had angel statutes all over and colorful couches and curtains. She told me I had many angels around me. Marti then asked me if I was gifted. I was not sure what she meant at first, and she told me she had a strong sense or something about me. I told her that I sometimes have bad dreams that later come to life and become a reality; it's almost as though I predicted a disaster. This has happened numerous times since I was a little girl. Marti then asked if this still happens to me, and I told her yes but not as often.

She then asked if I had three kids. I told her I did, but not anymore. She then heard "Hi, I am Ty" as clear as can be. He was trying to tell her that he was there and had been sick, and that it had something to do with his blood. Marti at first thought it was cancer, and I told her no. Ty told her it was not diabetes, and he told her this twice. He kept trying to explain that he had been choking. Marti said he was in a lot of pain and took a lot of medicine, and I told her yes, this was correct. She asked if he died from the medicine, and I told her I did not think so. I then explained to Marti about Behcet's syndrome.

Ty started talking about his dog to Marti, so she asked if Ty had a dog. I told her he did not die alone; his dog was with him. Marti said also there was a man in the house, correct? I told her yes, my husband, Marc, who was nursing a broken back down the hall in a back bedroom, was home at the time.

Marti asked me if Ty had an older sister and when I said yes, she said they were very close, and I said yes, best friends. Marti also spoke about a child in passing, and I believed she was speaking of a child of Chanti's whom she miscarried.

Ty told Marti that I go in his bedroom all the time, and that I have not changed it. He said someone lies in his bed, and Marti asked if I do that. I told her that I do at times, but I said his sister Chanti sleeps in his bedroom when she comes to visit us.

Ty told Marti I was wearing some clothing of his, a jacket or a sweatshirt of sorts, and he didn't want me to give it away. He was concerned because I had taken it off. I told Marti I went to pick up his dog, Yuba, and got hair all over his sweatshirt, so I took it off before I came to meet her.

Unexpectedly, Ty mentioned the name Jared, and Marti asked who he was. Later he mentioned Ed. These were both friends of his. They were both very good friends of Ty's for many years and like family to Marc and me. I felt they were like our children along with Ty, as they all grew up together. Ty was excited that I was there with Marti, and at the same time, he was getting frustrated with her, as he seemed to have so much he wanted to get across to her and me. Marti kept having to ask Ty to slow down, as he was so excitable. He actually was very funny at times also, just like when he was here with us on earth. He would say the same things to Marti that he would say to me here. It was unbelievable to me that this could be happening.

Ty told Marti that we were very close. He also told her that I was afraid of everything. He said he comes to see me at night and that he isn't far away from me.

Ty wanted me to know he had a job. He helps the children who die come across to the other side. Marti didn't know if this job was temporary or a long-term job. The kids were not afraid to die and cross over with Ty there for them. This did not surprise me, as Ty loved kids and was a kid at heart himself.

I asked Marti to ask Ty who greeted him from the other side when he passed. He said he was greeted by an older large woman, but there were a lot of people there besides her. Marti then asked if my mother was alive and I told her yes. We believed this woman to be my grandmother, Nanie. She asked where his memorial took place, and I told her the Chism House in Reno. Marti had never heard of it. She said Ty had many friends.

She also told me that Ty had lost several friends, one recently in a tragic death. I believe she was speaking of Kim (Brooke's best friend who over-dosed unintentionally from her prescription medication). Brooke was a pre-vious girlfriend of Ty's and they had lived together before Ty had met Sarah. Ty was very close to Kim and took her death very hard. When Ty was sick, he and Kim became close friends and they confided in one another. Ty did not have many friends when he was sick. He would run into Kim downtown while she was out walking on her break from work, and they would walk along the river and enjoy each other's company. Of course, neither knew they wouldn't be here much longer on this earth together, but they would meet again on the other side.

Ty told Marti that he had gone to McQueen High School. Marti said no other person has told her during her readings where they had gone to school. She found this to be very interesting.

I asked Ty if he was in any pain when he passed. He said it was like an ex-plosion that went off in his body and he was suddenly in this beautiful colorful place with everything so vividly green and beautiful with surrounding lakes and rivers. He was never scared or in pain.

During this visit, Ty also brought up his longtime girlfriend Sherril. They had known each other for years and had been together off and on over the years. She was a big part of Ty's growing up in Reno, and we all loved her very much. She was very much a part of our family.

He could not understand why people were upset and sad, when he was happy. Marti explained to him that he could come and go to this place on earth, but we could not do the same. Marti explained to me that Ty had no sense of time on the other side. For Ty, it seemed like he'd been gone for minutes, while I felt like he'd been gone a very long time. Ty could understand only how many seasons he had been gone. He knows seasons.

Marti said Ty has an ability that many people who cross over do not. He can actually move physical things in the house. I agreed with Marti that he is a very active soul. I have noticed things moving around, and I have seen Ty in his physical self. Marti said Ty comes to me a lot, usually at night. She said Ty is an old soul.

I also told Marti about the number twenty-nine being my favorite number all my life. I don't know why, as my son died at age twenty-nine, and I was twenty-nine when my father died. My dad was fifty-eight years old when he died, which is twenty-nine times two. Figure that? I was married on two/nine, back to that twenty-nine number. I could go on and on with that number but it definitely must mean something. I was a small child when this number was my favorite. Marti said our lives are mapped out for us before we are incarnated, and that is something we have in our "blueprints."

She told me that Ty would come to me in many ways. For instance, he might appear as birds, mainly hawks. I told her he does. She asked about the license plate thing. What does it mean? I told her I had a personalized plate, "MISSUTY," "miss you Ty." I also explained that Ty has been leaving me signs through other people's license plates. He lets me know he is thinking about me and that he is never far away.

Marti said Ty has touched many people and writes beautifully. This is so very true. I told her that Ty wrote music with his band.

Marti asked if Ty had a sister named Sarah. Ty kept saying Sarah's name repeatedly, and I told Marti, no, she was Ty's girlfriend when he left this place. She found Ty dead, along with Yuba lying in his bed beside him.

Ty told Marti I had a sister with lung cancer. He told her all about my sister's illness. The cancer had actually started in Jan's stomach and metastasized to her lung. It is a very slow cancer, and she is very ill. Marti had no way of knowing this information beforehand.

He also told Marti I could not sing. He would say all sorts of crazy things like this, but it was so like Ty. Ty and I often took road trips together to California to see family when Marc could not get time off from work. We would listen to music and sing. Yep, he's right, I cannot sing. Remember when I told you about the La La La song? Well, evidently Ty has not forgotten! It was as though he was sitting right there next to Marti, looking at me, and the three of us were having a conversation—with Ty back here with us on earth.

Ty asked several times how long he had been gone. Marti explained to me once again that the dead do not know time, but they know seasons. So Marti explained to him how many seasons had gone by. Ty then told me my yard needed to be raked. That's my boy! Yes, it was wintertime.

I showed Marti a gift someone had placed in my mailbox at Thanksgiving. This was a tiny pewter box that opened up, and inside were four angels. They did not leave a note of any kind with this gift. Immediately Ty interrupted Marti and said a friend gave this to me. I never found out who gave it to me. I treasure this gift.

The two hours I spent with Marti went by so quickly. Being able to communicate with my son was one of the most incredible experiences of my life.

Who would have thought it was possible? He and Marti seemed to have a special bond, and he was so easy for Marti to read. It was unbelievable. I was in awe that this could even be happening, that I was able to talk to my son again. I miss Ty terribly and want him here, but I am so ever thankful he can communicate with me through Marti and that I can look forward to future visits.

Since his passing I have spoken to him every day, sometimes several times a day, praying for him and for myself, to help me get through the day and to help me be a better person. Even though I have other children I absolutely adore, I wake up and think of him, and I go to bed thinking of him. If I wake in the night I will try to place myself into a meditative state so that I can be with him. You just never get over the loss of someone you love so very much.

The relationship with Marti on that day was just the start of our friendship and Ty's with her.

I continue to talk to Ty every day and thank him for the special things he does for me. They mean everything to me. I pray for him that he is happy, and I am so glad he is now out of his pain. I am so grateful that I have found this wonderful connection with my son, and we can communicate.

For the first two years after his passing, I cried myself all the way to work each day. When I got to the fifth floor, the elevator door opened each morning, and I put on my happy face like nothing was wrong and went to work as usual. At lunch sometimes I cried on my way home to see Yuba, but I would do the same thing, put on the happy face once again before that elevator door opened. Nobody at work knew my pain, nor did I expect them to understand what I was going through. I just prayed and hoped for the next sign. The only happiness I felt during this time was because of the almost daily signs Ty gave Marc or me. Marc was getting signs all the time now, and we would share our experiences with each other at the end of the day. We did not feel comfortable sharing this with many other people, as they did not understand, nor did we expect them to. If others had not gone through something similar to what we went through, how could they relate.

My next visit with Marti was on March 15, 2010. Ty was very present from the beginning. There were some others in the room also, possibly a grandfather figure, but we were not sure, as Ty was doing all the talking that day.

I asked Marti to ask Ty who slept in his bed the past weekend, and Ty said his dog. Marti said no, silly, and he said yes, he did! I told Marti that Ty was right. Ty also said his girlfriend did, though he did not say Sarah's name.

Ty explained to Marti that he would bring music to me now in different ways than before. Ty told Marti that I changed his sheets recently because I was anal. I told her yes, last night. Silly guy, the things he brings up.

Marti asked me if Ty had a tattoo. I told her yes. After she tried several times to explain what kind of tattoo he had, she concluded that it was somewhat of a circular design on his spine. Then Marti said it was Ty's initials. I told her yes, it was, and I explained that it looked almost like a Chinese symbol. It amazed me how Ty explained this to Marti. Sometime later, all of Ty's band friends from Steve Dave got the same tattoo on some part of their bodies in Ty's memory.

My grandson Isaac said Ty came to him and taught him a song on the guitar about love and relationships. Isaac said he had never heard the song before Ty came to him and taught him how to play it. Marti told me that it is very common for small children to experience this beautiful gift. My grandson Isaac has informed me that one day when he is older he would like to get the same tattoo as Ty's.

During this particular visit, Ty mentioned his friend Ed again. He worries about him. Marti asked about their situation, and Ty said they had a falling-out before he passed, but Ed came to his memorial. I had recently run into Ed, and he told me he was distraught because his father had just passed away. He told me that he had dreams about Ty, and they had made amends through his dreams. I am so happy for this.

Before our meeting ended, Ty had really warmed up and was feeling very comfortable with Marti. He also told her how sick he had felt before he died and how he had stomach problems.

In the winter of 2009, I met a young woman in downtown Reno at a craft fair. It was very cold at the time. She created artwork with blown glass. Her name was Nicole, and we hit it off immediately. I asked her if she was able to make me a piece of jewelry that could hold my son's ashes. She said she had never done it before but that she would love to do it for me. I was so very excited about this, so I got her phone number and address and told her I would contact her later.

On January 19, 2010, I was reading, and Marc had fallen asleep on the couch. Yuba was asleep also. I looked up toward the front door and saw a man standing there. I was scared at first and tried to wake Marc, but he slept. The man was tall, wearing black pants and a white shirt. He looked like he was wearing a suit from the 1800s. He had a goatee and dark curly hair. He stared at me for about thirty seconds, then disappeared. I have not seen him since and don't know who he was. Could he be a friend of Ty's or maybe an angel or spirit guide? I don't know. He has not been back. I think if he were to come back again, I would be more prepared for it and welcome him. I don't believe Ty would allow him to come into our home if he were bad.

Ty paid me another visit on April 16, 2010. I was lying on the living room couch, recuperating from foot surgery, when I heard a loud noise. I looked up and Ty was standing in the hall. He was wearing his tan shorts and his red T-shirt that had yellow writing on it. He was just looking at me but never said anything to me. This only lasted maybe forty seconds.

On May 8, 2010, Chanti came up for the weekend to meet with Marti later that day. Chanti had never met Marti, and she was so excited. First, though, we were to meet with Nicole with Ty's ashes to finally make some jewelry.

Chanti and I met early with Nicole at her house. Nicole's studio was in her garage. Nicole showed us the beautiful jewelry she made. We each explained the shape of the pendants we wanted her to make for us. We wanted her to make several pieces: a couple for each of us, one for Isaac, one for Kari, and one for each of Chanti's two half-sisters.

Ty's ashes were in an unopened box. When I opened the box, the ashes blew into our faces and onto the couch in the garage where we were sitting. I thought to myself, this is Ty being silly and playing a joke on us. Ty was such a jokester. Nothing surprised me when it came to him. We all laughed about this. Good thing Nicole had a sense of humor. She felt extremely honored that we would ask her to do this for us, because she knew how much it meant to us. She had never been asked to do this for anyone before and was very excited about it. It was a wonderful day, and the three of us had a lot of fun.

After spending time and talking more with Nicole, Chanti and I learned that Nicole knew Ty from high school. They never hung out together in the same crowd, but they were acquaintances. What a small world, I thought. We left Nicole's and were to meet with her after the jewelry had been fired at a later date.

Chanti met with Marti that afternoon for the first time. Marti, of course, had no idea what Chanti and I had done earlier that morning. Immediately Marti asked Chanti, "So what's up with the ashes?" Nobody had ever told Marti what we were doing that morning. Marti asked if the ashes had blown away or if they had been split up. I think Chanti was in a bit of shock that Marti knew this. Chanti was somewhat skeptical of Marti, not having met her before and did not know what to think. Chanti has had her own experiences with Ty coming to her in dream visits. Even though Chanti has had these experiences with Ty, I think she still had a hard time believing. How can this be? Through Marti, Ty explained that Chanti and I had made some necklaces earlier that day with some of his ashes placed inside the pieces. These days, Nicole makes similar pieces of jewelry for others who have lost loved ones. She does so at no charge through hospice.

I always felt that my daughter was a little skeptical of my going to a medium, though we would talk about Marti all the time. I would tell Chanti about all the wonderful things I experienced with Ty through Marti, and some of my own personal experiences that I had throughout the day. This particular day was so special for both of us, and there was no way Marti could have known what we had planned to do earlier in the day. My boy once again came through and for both of us. Ty is a great communicator, and luckily, Marti can read him very well.

Chanti herself has had many experiences with Ty, mainly in dreams where she and Ty will be talking, and she will say, "Ty, how can you be here? You're dead." He will say yes and hold her hand or even hug her. Ty will explain to her that he is visiting. She will then beg him to please not let go, because she knows he will be gone again.

On Father's Day, June 2010, my brother Gary committed suicide. I received this horrible news from my younger brother, Jon. My family lived in the San Luis Obispo and Santa Barbara County area except for my sister, Jan, and we lived up in Reno. Marc and I had planned to drive down to see Gary and his wife, Cindy, that weekend. We knew Gary was having some health issues and was depressed by this, but we did not realize how bad his depression had become. We were looking forward to seeing them and the rest of the family during this visit. I spoke with Gary on the telephone once or twice a week, as we were very close, and I had hoped that we would one day live near one another to spend more time together when we all retired from our jobs. Unfortunately, this never happened.

I last spoke to Gary on the phone the week before Father's Day, and I knew that there was something just not right with him. When I got off the telephone with my brother, I told Marc, "My brother is not well." Little did I know he would do something so crazy as to end his life before we had a chance to come down and see him that coming weekend. It so saddens me that he did this. He was loved by everyone and is greatly missed. I don't think he realized what an impact he had on everyone.

My brother went into the back forty of his property, to a garage built for his boat that he loved so, and slipped inside an orange sleeping bag along with his shotgun and did the unthinkable. Oh, my gosh, how I wish I had seen my brother before this. Just maybe I could have made a difference in his life and his decision to leave it. I was angry at my brother for some time for doing something I felt was so foolish and unnecessary, but I have come to grips with his death now and forgiven him. Gary visits me also from time to time, and I now know he is very happy and glad to be where he is. I no longer feel anger, but I am sad that we could not have spent more time together in our later years, as I had hoped we would.

I lost my father, whom I loved greatly, my beautiful son, Ty, and now my brother Gary. Unfortunately, our family has not quite recovered from all this and has never been quite the same. These were three strong men in the family, and now they are all gone. I was close to all three of them, and this about killed me. I always felt I would have my brother and son here for support if anything were to happen to my husband before I pass. They were my rock and now they're gone.

August 5, 2010, was Ty's thirtieth birthday. It was a year after Ty passed away. While driving that day on our way to the lake to spread Ty's ashes at his favorite place, two hawks flew right over our truck. I said, "There's Ty and Gary."

Marc, Chanti, Isaac, Kari, Sarah, and Jess, Ty's best friend, all went out on our boat that day. It was a quiet but nice day on the lake. We toasted champagne to Ty and sang songs while enjoying the warm sun of the day. My son-in-law, Merritt, stayed at home with my two other grandsons this day, as there was only so much room on the boat.

Later, we came home and had a birthday party for Ty at the house. We had a nice barbecue and a few of Ty's good friends came, played guitar, and sang. It was a lovely evening. Oh, how I miss the music in our house. Ty was always playing guitar, and if not, he was playing the piano. His friends were always around, and the house was full of people, so very uplifting.

After Marc and I had gone to bed that evening, I got up to get a drink of water. I felt a swirl of wind around me, like someone had rubbed across my back. I am sure it was Ty, thanking me for his party, as he loved parties.

It seems like Ty tries to be here for me when I need him the most, especially during special times like birthdays, anniversaries, or Christmas. Ty is always very present and right on within days of those special occasions. I look forward to them and the surprises he will have in store for me. He may not always have the exact day, but he knows his seasons!

Ty was so very close to both Marc and me, and it is as if Ty is sitting in the living room with us every night, discussing every event occurring within our lives. We did so much together every day. He is ever present in our lives every day, just differently now. I thank Ty over and over for what we have shared and our connection with one another. If it were not for Ty being there for me and guiding me through my everyday life, it would all be so much more difficult for me. Of course, I would rather have him back in the physical self, but this is what I have for now. I look forward to the times I see him in his physical form. I am so grateful for what he has given me to move forward. We will never forget him, and he knows that. Ty is always with me. He has shown me that he really isn't that far away from us, just in another realm or dimension. He's taught me so much about life and death. I was always afraid to die, but I know now that you never truly die, and life does not end; it just changes once you shed your physical self. I am no longer afraid. It's like moving onto a new adventure. Something we work toward our whole life, and when we leave this place called earth, we can now be at peace with the world and ourselves.

Ty has also taught me to be more tolerant and patient with others. Something I have always had to work on. To accept others for who they are and not judge them is a really hard thing to do. I saw how others judged Ty. They did not know what he was going through and did not believe he was sick. You never know what turmoil one may be going through in life, and it is so easy to judge when you are not involved in someone else's daily life. Life is precious, and it can be so difficult when it's taken away from you in an instant. I believe we are all here for a reason and to learn life's lessons. Lessons to be learned are different for each person.

I went to see Marti after my brother passed. I was hoping Gary would come through but was not sure that it would happen. Before my brother passed and I talked to him about my seeing Marti and communicating with Ty, I think Gary thought I was off my rocker! Anyway, I hoped Gary would come through on this visit.

Ty came to Marti in the early morning hours before my appointment time, something he does quite often before my visits with Marti. He just gets so excited that I'm coming to see him. Marti has told me that when he appears early like that she has to first question who it is. When she finally realizes it is Ty, she will look at her calendar, and sure enough, I am on her calendar for that day. She tells Ty that she will see him later on, but not at that moment; he has to wait. This is so amazing to me. My boy just loves Marti and her ability to bring us together. This visit was incredible.

Marti said that Gary appeared to be next to Ty. He was very confused at first about Marti and me being there. This was all new to Gary, and Marti explained who she was. She told him she could read him, and we could communicate with each other through her. Ty told Gary he would show him how this thing works! It was pretty funny actually. Gary caught on pretty well and thought it interesting we could communicate, and our visit went smoothly from there. Gary's spirit was pretty active, like Ty's. Marti could read Gary very well. In the physical world both Ty and Gary had type A personalities! Everyone loved them both, and did I mention how handsome they both were?

Through Marti, I asked Gary if he ever felt pain when he committed suicide. He said no. He told me he was very happy now, that he was in pain while on earth. He said it was his time to go. Marti spoke up and said she didn't know my brother had a beard. I told Marti that Gary usually shaved his beard off in the summer months, but he wore a beard most of the time.

Gary told Marti he spends a lot of time fishing with our dad, and that Dad is building a new boat. He also spends time with his friend who passed away, whose name is also Gary. He spoke of the condos in Lake Tahoe, vacationing there with all the family, and the good times we had there. He felt bad for leaving the way he did but said he could not take it anymore. I don't remember too much of this particular visit, as it was so emotional for me, but since that time, my brother has come through on numerous occasions when I have gone to see Marti.

These days I often find myself praying to both Ty and Gary. I feel they help me get through difficult days, and I have many of those. To me they are my angels, and they keep me grounded. When I need guidance, I ask them for their help, and they give me answers. I have asked for their help when I was not sure I could trust someone, and they have told me whether I could trust the person. The dead do not lie. I always thank them for their guidance and pray that their souls are free and they are happy. I have to believe that they are because they tell me they are.

Even though I have an ongoing relationship with my son who is on the other side, I receive so much valuable information from my friend Marti when I see her, that I have continued to see her about every two or three months. I always have so much going on in my life, and it is so nice to hear Ty talk about all the things going on with me and showing me that he is right alongside me while I am going through all the different things in my daily life. I treasure every moment.

Although Marti is a medium and a psychic, I believe she truly is a life coach; she most certainly has been to me. She has taught me so much over the years, and I believe that Ty brought us together for a reason. I feel safe, trust her unconditionally, and I have found a wonderful friend in Marti. Some people may choose to go see a psychiatrist, and that is great, but I feel very comfortable where I am during this time of my life.

My grandson Isaac was extremely close to Ty. He was six years old when Ty passed. When Chanti was going through a divorce, Ty spent a lot of time with the two of them and was like a father figure to Isaac. Ty had hoped he would get well enough to move to California and live down there with the two of them. Unfortunately, that never happened. Isaac has expressed to his mom and me that he would like to have a visit with Marti. I am hoping for this to take place in the near future, but we have not been able to yet because of the distance and timing involved in his coming. It will happen one day.

Ty comes to see Isaac. The first time he came to see Isaac he had been in his bed at night. Isaac could see clearly through Ty's body like he was a skeleton. He could see the blood running through his bones, and it frightened him. He was only six years old at the time. After Isaac told me about this experience, I asked Ty during one of my visits with Marti if he could come to Isaac the way he appears to me in his physical form so as not to scare him. Ty never appeared to Isaac like that again. Ty would never have wanted to scare Isaac, and I am sure he had no idea he was scaring him when he appeared before him.

Now, when Ty comes to see Isaac, he sometimes dresses almost clown-like, wearing funny ties, while standing on the side of the road while his mother and he are driving. Ty will just be off to the side of the road smiling at them. He will do silly things just like when he was here in his physical self.

Another time Isaac saw his uncle Ty in a bathroom stall reading a book with his feet propped up against the wall as if he was lounging in there. Isaac said he walked into a restroom at a restaurant and saw him there, just out of the blue! Isaac walked out laughing aloud, and his mom asked what was up. Isaac explained what Ty had done. Isaac treasures these times he sees his uncle Ty. He looked silly and makes Isaac laugh. Isaac is no longer afraid to see Ty. Isaac is so much like Ty. He's not like Ty was as a child; he's the way Ty was as an adult. They definitely have a connection.

Chanti has since remarried and has another child, Satori, who also sees her uncle Ty. She never met Ty on earth, as she was born years after Ty passed. Ty will come to Satori and she tells her mom, "See, Mama, Uncle Ty, look. He's sleeping on a cloud." Chanti has never told Satori that Ty is in heaven. To this day she still talks about him as if he is in the room. Satori has seen pictures of Ty, and on her way downstairs to her bedroom at night to go to sleep, she says good night to him every night.

It was September 20, 2010, my first birthday after Ty passed. I asked Ty to please give me a sign that he was still with me. Even though I know in my heart he is with me, I always felt like I needed his validation that he was still here and would never leave me.

I had taken the day off work and had just had a shower. Marc and I were going out later for dinner that night. The doorbell rang, and I thought it was strange that somebody would be coming over. It was Ty's girlfriend Sherril from years ago. What a nice surprise. Ty and Sherril were kids when they got together, and they spent a lot of time together over the years. They were in and out of each other's lives. We always loved Sherril.

She told me she had some pictures of Ty she had taken in 2002 while in a photography class in college. They were duplicate pictures that were at her mom's house, and she thought I would like them. Sherril did not know it was my birthday; she thought I would be at work. When she came to the house, she had planned to leave the pictures at the front door. Sherril and I had a very nice visit, and she told me how Ty comes to her in her dreams. I told her that he will always love her and one day they will be together, but that she needed to go on with her life with her new husband. This about killed me saying this to her, as I loved her so much, but I knew this was the best thing for her—not to stay in love with a dead man.

I could not have received a nicer gift than this on my birthday. I always loved her and thought Ty and Sherril one day would have been married and had their own children. To have her show up this day was so special to me.

Visit with Marti Tote on October 24, 2010

I told Marti that Ty gave me a beautiful birthday present this year. Ty told Marti he gave me a dead person. Marti did not want to tell me what Ty said, and I told her, to just tell me. Marti apologized to me later, but I was not offended, as I know what a goofball Ty is. I just wanted to know what he said. He was trying to explain that his old girlfriend brought a picture of him, something about his eyes and hair. I told Marti that this was all correct. Sherril had stopped by with some photos of Ty. This was Ty's way of explaining to us about my gift. He came through once again! These beautiful pictures are hanging in my house. I am ever so thankful to Sherril for that day, as she had no idea what these pictures and her visit meant to me.

I do feel they are soul mates and will meet up again one day. They loved each other very much over many years, and I feel it was all about the timing. Unfortunately, it was never right in this lifetime.

My brother Gary came through during one of my visits with Marti on October 24, 2010. Gary said he was excited that he was going to be a grandfather for the first time. Marti asked if Gary had a son. Through Marti, Gary said yes. Gary said he knew that Aubri, his daughter-in-law, was pregnant before Brian, his son, knew about the baby. Marti thinks the baby is a boy. Gary knows what the sex of the baby is but will not say. Later, Aubri and Brian had a son they named Jax. Gary was so excited about Jax having been born. He spends a lot of time around Jax and the family.

I told Marti that Ty comes to visit me all the time, and she said yes, he does. She said that he spends a lot of time at our house, which is unusual, as most spirits do not have this bond with their past. He loved it here and likes to be with both Marc and me. She said he will never leave us.

Ty began to talk about a tattoo but Marti already knew that Ty had a tattoo. Gary came through during this particular visit and spoke of the tattoo also. It was funny, as they were both so excited about a tattoo. It took a while during this session but what they were trying to tell us finally came through.

Gary was very present during this reading, and he told us that his son, Brian, had a new tattoo. They were both excited about this. Marti could not see the tattoo until she asked Gary to step aside a minute. As Ty is so easy for Marti to read, she asked for his help to show her the tattoo on Brian's upper body. The tattoo is an exact picture of Gary in detail below Brian's heart. Marti could see Gary's picture tattooed on Brian's chest and said what a beautiful man he was. Marti had never seen a picture of Gary before. She said what a beautiful family we had. She then told me she would give anything to bring Ty back to me for just one day. She said she could not imagine losing a child.

I asked Marti during this visit if Gary was sad. Gary said he was ready to go when he left us and was now out of pain. She said both he and Ty are happy and surrounded by family and friends. Ty is always telling Marti how many friends he has on the other side. When they see us sad, they do not understand it because they are here with us, though we do not see them. I have been told that spirits can be in more than one place at a time.

Ty brought up the names Steve and Greta. My neighbors across the street are Steve and Grace. I believe Ty was talking about them. Ty played guitar and so does Steve, and Grace is a singer. They knew one another when Ty was alive, and they moved across the street from us after Ty had passed away. Ty said they were having a baby, a girl. This was in October 2010, and I started writing *Ty's Story* in September 2014. They came to tell me a few weeks ago they are having a baby girl in November. The dead never lie.

February 9, 2011, was our twenty-sixth wedding anniversary. I was missing Ty very much and speaking aloud to him. Something I do almost every day. It was lunchtime, and I was on my way home from work. Two hawks flew over my car and circled above me while I was driving. I was driving back to work on Arlington after lunch when a large hawk flew over my car again as I was driving. I know Ty was letting me know that he was thinking of me.

On February 10, 2011, my dad came to visit me in a dream. I had been praying for two weeks that he would come see me. He looked very well other than a little wrinkled around his eyes. He has beautiful turquoise eyes and black hair. Not a very tall man, but husky with large hands. He had a very nice build on him. My mother would always say that. My dad was wearing a red nylon-type shirt and light-blue pants. In my dream, we were talking back and forth, and I asked him why he didn't come to see me. We stood face-to-face. As I looked at him, I noticed a tear in his left eye. Then he disappeared and went back to wherever it is he goes. When I awakened, I was so happy to have had this dream visit with my dad.

I had been having numerous experiences with Ty on a daily basis. It was October 2011, and I was about to have another foot surgery. I was not feeling well that day and stayed home from work. It was midmorning, the house was very quiet, and I heard a cough. There was nobody in the house but me, so I started to talk to Ty. I asked if he was there in the room with me.

Later that afternoon, I was reading in my chair in the living room area, and I noticed Ty at the front door. He was standing outside the glass door looking at me. I could see him plainly, as if he were "alive" and getting ready to walk through the front door into the house. He was wearing tan shorts and a white T-shirt. I told him that I knew he was with me, as I felt his presence around me that day, and he just smiled at me. He stayed for about forty-five seconds, which seemed like a much longer time than that. Yuba came into the room, dropped his ball from his mouth as if he saw him too, and ran to the front door as if to greet him. I know he sees Ty.

After my foot surgery, I was home recouping and felt the need to keep busy, though I was supposed to be off my feet! I grabbed my 2012 calendar and proceeded to write important dates on it for the next year. As I was writing on the calendar and came to the date October 12, the date of Ty's passing, outside I heard a hawk squawking quite loudly as if it was trying to get my attention. Is this a coincidence, or was Ty the hawk, letting me know he was there with me?

On December 31, 2011, Marc and I decided to take Yuba for a walk late in the afternoon. It was a beautiful day and fairly warm. There had been a fire at Thanksgiving time up the street from us, and someone had lost their home. We decided to walk in that direction to see what horrible damage had occurred. I just remember thinking of how sad I was for the poor homeowner, and how fortunate we were that we had made it through the fire.

Ty was heavily on my mind. He still had not shown me anything significant that would have stood out more than usual to me, as some sort of Christmas gift or something to let Marc and me know he was thinking of us during this holiday season. I felt a little sad. Ty was such a kid at Christmas that we still gave him a Christmas stocking. I always told the kids that if they believed in Santa, he would come! They were not going to not believe in Santa!

We ended up walking in the ditch trail up above our neighborhood, and I suddenly heard a hawk above us. Then we noticed that there were two hawks up above and they followed Marc, Yuba, and me as we headed back toward home. They circled above us, then flew toward the sunset, came around us, and circled above us again. I believed they wanted us to know they were there with us. They were very verbal also. They seemed to be dancing in the sun. It was a beautiful sight. For a moment I wished I were a hawk, flying up above in this beautiful sunset. They looked so peaceful. They stayed within our sight until we could no longer see them because the sun was in our eyes. They were probably above us for a good half hour while we walked along the path.

As we were walking, we noticed the sagebrush and trees along our pathway had been decorated with shiny Christmas balls placed about every ten feet. Glass balls of different colors and shapes appeared before us as we walked along the path, which seemed like a city block long. They were beautiful. That day was such a special day for the two of us, one we would treasure forever. Whoever placed the balls there had no idea what this meant to us. Sometimes it is just the little signs that make this world so special.

On that afternoon, I got my gift, or sign, from my son that he was with me. Marc and I had a choice to go one of two ways on our path to get home, and we chose this particular one, which happened to have the decorative balls placed on the trees. Had we chosen to go on the other pathway, we would never have seen the beautiful sight before us and received our sign that Ty wanted us to see that day.

I spoke to Marti in a visit sometime afterward about what had transpired on our walk. She told me that Ty did not place the balls on the bushes for us to see, but he put a message in my head so that I would choose the pathway that would lead us to where we would see the balls that were hanging on the bushes! That's my boy. He is such a communicator, and I love him for that.

Ty is good about making sure I know he is thinking of Marc and me when it comes to important dates in our lives. He might not always have it on the exact date, but he will have the week down. He is always close. He knows how I plan and how I work, and he is so in tune with me. I am thankful for everything he shares with me.

It was a Friday at the end of July 2012 that Marc and I both took the day off and took Yuba with us to Lake Stampede for the day. We had the whole beach to ourselves, and Yuba loved being able to run around in the water and chase birds, lizards, and whatever else he could find. We could hardly keep him out of the water. We barely took the boat out onto the lake that day; we just enjoyed hanging out on the shore, enjoying the beauty and sunshine of that day.

Behind where we were sitting, I kept hearing the chirping of a bird. As I turned around, I noticed there was a large, quite long log with a little yellow bird sitting on it. It was as though the bird was trying to get our attention, as he was verbal and loud. Yuba went running over to it, and the weird thing is the bird never moved. This bird was not afraid of Yuba, and it would try to get closer to him. The bird would move a few feet, stop and look at Yuba, and just stare at him. It was the strangest thing. I always felt Ty came around in the form of a hawk, but maybe just this day he became a different kind of bird. This went on for some time. This bird definitely wanted us to know he was there and was not afraid of us.

On another occasion, I was at a stop sign on my way home from work at lunchtime, coming home to see Yuba, when a small yellow bird landed on the hood of my car. Twice now a yellow bird has appeared before me. I don't know exactly what it means, but it definitely has gotten my attention.

I was getting close to Christmastime 2012, and I wondered what Ty would do special for Marc and me that year. It had been extremely windy during that time before Christmas, and we would take our regular walks with Yuba, making sure to dress warmly, as it was so cold. One day I noticed this silver object at the far end of an old white wooden fence at the far end of someone's property line. I glanced at it but didn't really take it all in at that moment. We walked by that shiny object for two weeks when finally, I walked over and picked it up. It was a plastic silver Christmas ornament, quite large, about thirteen inches long, the type of ornament you would hang outside on a tree. I picked it up and took it home, cleaned it up, and hung it up in our living room along with our other hanging balls at Christmas. I BELIEVE this was our gift from Ty this year.

I had a visit with Marti sometime after taking the ornament home, and in that reading, Ty said he had given me a long silver shiny ornament for Christmas. Ty is such a good communicator; he never fails me.

During my many visits with Ty, he has explained to me that even though he spends a lot of time with me, his sisters, his niece, nephew, etc., he can do this because he consists of energy with no physical body—he can be in more than one place at the same time. He can just think of something and be there or have it appear before him.

Ty sometimes comes to me as a child in my dreams and is only about four years old. I was talking to him and asking him if he would please come to me as an adult in my dream. In April of 2013, he came to me in a dream. I was so excited and said, "Ty, you finally came to me." I don't remember much of the dream other than our conversation. He told me that he knew he had passed away, but he was just visiting me. What I find strange about this incident is my mother was in part of the dream that night also. My mother is very much alive and in her eighties, but she appeared to me as very young and pretty. Also, in my dream, I had lost all my hair! Wow, now what could all this mean? It was pretty stressful.

My daughter often has these kinds of dreams with her brother, in which they are together talking, maybe holding hands or hugging, and she tells him to not let go because she is afraid he will leave. She will say to Ty, "But you're dead. How can you be here? He tells her, "Yes, I know, but I am just visiting."

On May 14, 2013, I received an e-mail from Marti, saying that someone was trying to get her attention regarding my mother. She asked me what was going on. I told her my mother had pancreatitis and was soon having surgery to have her gall bladder removed. I told Marti my mother has lost a lot of weight, and

Marti was concerned about my mother's kidneys. About this time, I made an appointment to see Marti.

We had been trying to sell our boat for a couple of years. It was difficult for us to continue going to the lake without Ty being here with us. I asked Ty during that visit if we were ever going to sell the boat. Ty told me we would sell the boat only when the right family came along. Eventually, we sold it to a young couple with two kids, a boy and girl.

Ty used to come to me quite often in his physical form in the middle of the night. I'd wake up, walk into the bathroom, get a glass of water, and he would be to my left, standing at the opening to my walk-in closet. One night he frightened me in the dark, and he has not come back to this location since. I pray to him that he will come back. I let him know that he startled me that night, but I don't want him to stay away from me. I want to continue to see him in his physical form. Since then, he is bringing me other loved ones who have passed on, and I can see them clearly.

Sometimes at night, I awake from a sound sleep because the bed is shaking. I look over at Marc, and he is fast asleep. Immediately, my thoughts go to Ty. I believe he is trying to get my attention.

One morning Marc opened his jewelry box, which sits on his dresser. Inside was a one-hundred-dollar bill that had not been there previously. We have no idea where that came from. I told Marc that Ty might have given it to him for his birthday. Marc said maybe, and just then, after I had said that to Marc, a glass hummingbird ornament hanging in our entryway fell to the floor and broke into numerous pieces. I believe this was a sign from our son to let us know once again he is with us, and just maybe, he had something to do with that hundred-dollar bill!

My experiences with my son continue almost daily. One day, I went to put on my wedding ring, and it was gone. When I take it off, I always set it in the same place. I was so distraught by this, and I had to leave for work before I could find it. I was so upset, and I prayed I would find it. I asked for Ty's help while at work that day. I came home later that day during lunch to see Yuba, which was a normal thing for me to do at lunch, and something just made me go to this particular jewelry box of mine where I put only my bracelets and necklaces. I have never placed rings inside this before, but something made me look inside. There inside was my ring. I was shocked by this. I don't know how it got there, nor do I remember placing it inside. After this, I walked outside to change Yuba's pool water—yes, he has his own pool! A butterfly flew up close to me and I kind of backed up, as it almost landed in my hand. Crazy, but I see this as a sign from my son, as he helped me discover a way to find my ring and helped me once again. I love that amazing boy...

Marc and I had been preparing for a trip to visit our dear friends in Pennsylvania, and this came up in a reading as if Ty was planning this trip right along with us. Through a reading with Marti, he said we were taking a trip, that we would be near a large lake, and that he was very excited for us. Our friends live a block from Lake Erie! Ty has learned to communicate so well.

Two years after my son passed away from this horrible disease, Behcet's syndrome, I received a letter in the mail from Social Security Disability that my son had been awarded Disability and Medicaid, which would pay for his medical expenses. I cannot tell you how angry this makes me feel. Had he received this health insurance/disability income earlier on, instead of having to wait two years, doctors could have saved his life. The system grossly failed him. I believe the government made Ty wait this thing out so long because he was so young; they would have been paying for him for a long time, and they did not want to do that, as it would have cost them too much money.

About a year after Social Security paid me back what was owed to Ty, they sent me a letter requesting I send them money back, as they claimed they overpaid me. I was not going to fight them on this and just wanted to get on with my life. I wrote them a check for the amount they requested. Six months after I did so, they said I never paid and requested another check from me. Fortunately, I kept good records of their mistake. I sent them a copy of the check I originally sent them. I never heard from them again regarding Ty.

I've asked Ty if he can call me on the telephone and somehow communicate to me that it is he. Ty has told me through Marti that he is very good with electronics and that on a landline telephone he could, because he is energy, and electronics is energy. Being a musician and having been in several bands over the years, Ty always liked electronics. I have told him on numerous occasions to please come to me—I want to hear his voice!

I find that he likes to mess around with my television in the living room and my stereo equipment, especially when I am playing CDs. Sometimes, when I am in the middle of typing on the computer in my computer room, Ty's picture will just pop up out of nowhere on my screen. Before I retired from work, he used to do that same little trick, however he does it. I would be in the middle of a project, and there he would appear on my screen, and I would be looking at him. It was crazy that he could do that, but he would make my day.

Sometimes I will go to my cell phone and his phone number will just pop up with his name. No, I have never erased his phone number from my phone though someone else now has his number. I cannot get myself to erase it from my phone.

I woke up from a dream visit from Ty in the middle of the night, and after I explained what it was like to Marti, she told me that Ty had kept me on the other side too long. She said when we dream of someone who has passed away, we are actually going to them, not the reverse. On this particular visit, I woke up feeling sick, as if I had thick blood or something the consistency of "thick meat" in my throat as if I was going to choke or vomit. I could almost see it, as it felt so thick! It was the most horrible feeling, and I will never forget it. This has never happened to me again. I beg Ty to take me to the place where he is, but I think he is too afraid I won't want to come back here, so either he does not take me there, or I do not remember our dream visits together.

For several years, I have enjoyed a close connection with my son and grown closer to Marti. My son has been able to communicate so very well and bring other family members to me. Most of the time this happens during visits with Marti, but I have had visits from family members who have passed, and Marti was not around. I have seen them as if they were standing right in front of me.

I had major surgery in February 2014, and I had not been feeling well afterward. I had been watching the program on television called *Long Island Medium*. This episode was about a couple who lost their son twenty-one years ago at the age of three and a half. As I was watching this, my telephone rang, and I answered it. Whoever was on the other end just listened to my voice, then hung up. I believe it was Ty, letting me know he was thinking about me. I could not help but wonder if this was maybe my time to leave this place.

One evening in March 2014, I was reading a book while sitting in my chair. I saw something in the corner of my eye and looked up at the front door. Ty was standing at the door. I saw him clearly. I turned to Marc and told him Ty was here visiting. Just then, I heard a cracking sound and a large houseplant, which was beside me, dropped a branch onto the wood floor. Wow, that got my attention!

A few weeks afterward, I asked Ty if he would please come to me or in a dream; I needed to hear his voice. The very next day I heard Ty talking in the entryway. It was as if he was trying to speak with me while I was in another room. At first, I went to see if Marc was talking, but I soon realized he was in the shower and it was definitely not him. I was hearing Ty's voice.

I find that I do not usually remember my dreams when Ty is in them. When I do remember them, most of the time Ty appears in my dreams as a small child.

I scheduled a visit with Marti in May.

Visit with Marti Tote on May 5, 2014

This was a particularly interesting visit with Marti. I told her I had not been feeling well since my surgery. Both Ty and Gary appeared immediately. For the first time, my grandmother, Nanie, appeared and she was telling me I would be OK; I just needed to change my diet. She was so anxious to tell Marti how she had passed. The dead love to tell you that information, according to Marti. Nanie told us she did not die alone and she was not at home; her heart gave out. I told Marti this was all true. My mother and I were with Nanie when she passed away, and her heart finally gave out. She had been in the hospital. Before she left us, she spoke softly to us about the dark tunnel. Then she saw her mother, whom she left so many years ago in Holland when she came to the United States, and Nanie started speaking in Dutch to her. Moments later, she left us...

What I found so amazing was that my grandmother passed away twenty-seven years ago on May 5, 2014, and she had never appeared to me before this date. Ty told me that she was there for him when he crossed over to the other side. It was so special that she came to me after such a long time. I had such a wonderful visit with my grandmother that day. We had spent a lot of time together and were very close when she was alive.

There were many people around Nanie, as if something was getting ready to happen, possibly another death, somebody coming home...It was like a family reunion or party. My grandfather, Papa, was there as were Marc's father, Bob, and his aunt Marcella. I had never had a visit with Marti such as this before with so many relatives coming through all together. Relatives who had never met one another here on earth were all congregated together and wanting to talk all at once. My father's biological dad, whom he had never met before, was with him also. It was unbelievable.

During this visit I asked Marc's father if Marc's stepmother, Marlene, was OK. He said she was not well. I found out a week after my visit with Marti that Marlene had been in the hospital for a hemorrhage.

My father's mother, Nana, who lived to be over 101 years old, even appeared. She was talking up a storm! She spoke of how she loved to wear hats and talked about her retirement from the motion picture industry. She had been a seamstress and she used to sing. As a young child, she used to make beautiful clothes for my sister, Jan, and me. Nana was feisty as long as I could remember, and was the same on the other side as when she was here with us. She spoke of not liking my mother and spitting on her! Yikes...

It was about three weeks after this visit, on June 1, 2014, that my uncle Ralph passed away. I believe all my family members who had passed on were there waiting for my uncle to join them when I was there during my visit with Marti. They were all getting ready for my uncle Ralph to join them, and they were all celebrating his homecoming. I am so glad that people who leave this place never die alone and are well taken care of. The ones left behind are the ones who are sad and have such a hard time going on with their lives.

I asked Ty if it was different for him now from when he first left us. He told me he feels more settled and at home. Whenever I tried to ask Ty something, Nanie would jump in and starting telling Marti stuff, like how she used to love to wear colorful housecoats with big pockets. This is so true. She and Marti got along well and she was so easy for Marti to read. She even went into detail about how she was a larger woman with big breasts! Yep, that's my grandma. She was a very sweet woman. As a child, she was not a healthy person. In spite of heart problems, she lived a long, beautiful life and everyone loved her.

I asked Ty if he knew night from day on earth. He said he could only tell this by when we go to sleep.

Ty always finds some way of letting me know he is close to me. Whether he brings his physical being to me, calls me up in a dream, or leaves me the many signs he shows me. It happened to be the fifth anniversary of his passing. I kept looking for any sign that he was with me. I did not want to stay home that day, and I wanted to keep busy. Marc and I left early in the morning, driving to Apple Hill in Placerville, California, to visit the farms and go wine tasting. It was horribly busy when we arrived, which made us a little crazy. Since it was not so enjoyable, we decided we had to get away from it all.

Therefore, we went wine tasting and had lunch. It was a wonderful day after we made that decision to leave the farms, and we couldn't have asked for better weather that day. We met nice people everywhere we stopped, and it was not crowded at the wineries. A nice day to get away and take our mind off things for a bit. I am sure Ty was "sitting in our backseat" while we were traveling, and he was wine tasting right along with us. He loved to go wine tasting with us. Nothing too eventful happened that day. Unusual for my son not to give us a big sign of some sort.

The next day I was walking Yuba and talking to Ty as usual. Something I do every morning and throughout the day, asking for advice or just telling him how much I appreciate him and love him. I asked him to help me with his story.

Yuba and I got home from our morning walk. It was 9:00 a.m. on Monday, October 13, 2014. My telephone rang, and the person on the other side hesitated and then said, "It's me!" Could this be my son? This was Ty's voice speaking to me. It had to be Ty. Oh my gosh, this is so exciting and hopefully this is the start of a new communication from the other side. We were then disconnected.

Yesterday was his special day. The day someone dies is their true birthday and Ty loves a party! I am sure my brother Gary was right along with him partying. Ty could not have given me a nicer gift than to call me and for me to hear his voice one more time.

VISIT WITH MARTI ON OCTOBER 15, 2014

Marti told me she had been on vacation for a week in Southern California with family during the five-year anniversary of Ty's passing. When Marti returned, she posted something so beautiful on Facebook. Something to the effect that Ty had brought his parents to her and we have become friends. She thanked Ty for finding her. She said she did not miss him, because she did not have to lose him. It was not her loss, but that they have shared many secrets together and have a special relationship.

Ty had come to Marti, explaining to her that she should think about what she was posting. He worried about his mother's reputation; he wondered what people would think if they did not "believe." Marti had ended her post with the phrase "band of angels." Ty kept telling Marti and me during our visit he wanted her to end her posting with "Rock On." Marti did not know why he would say that and if it had any significance to me. I told her it did.

I explained to Marti that last year when we went to Cleveland, Ohio to the Rock and Roll Hall of Fame we discovered you can purchase a memorial brick in your loved one's name and have written whatever you want on same. The stones are cemented in a circle in front of the Hall of Fame building. We were to end Ty's with "Rock On." We felt this would be appropriate since our son was a musician and what better place to have a memorial? We did not have the opportunity to do this during our visit to Cleveland at that time, but since have purchased Ty's memorial stone in his memory at the Rock and Roll Hall of Fame. Marti was amazed by this. Ty is a very good communicator.

We talked about how Marti can feel Ty and know it is him but does not hear his voice. She asked Ty if he could hear her voice and he said no. She told me that she has professionally worked in this field for nine years and this question had never popped up before this time.

I told her that I have been seeing dead people, but I think I have also heard them. I told her that it was people I know who have passed and she said, "Of course." I reminded her of a visit I had with her when we had asked Ty if he could call me on a telephone and I was told he could but only on a landline telephone. He said he could because a telephone is electronics. He consists of energy and electronics is energy.

I explained to Marti that I received a telephone call that I believed was from Ty. She then asked Ty, "Did you call your mother?' He said yes. Marti asked Ty what he said to me. Ty said, "Hey, it's me, I love you." I only heard Ty say, "It's me," but I never heard him say "hey" or "I love you." When I told Marti what Ty said to me she was amazed by this. Then Ty asked if his voice sounded like him. I told him yes. Marti thinks my soul's connection to him is so strong that he needs to be around me. I feel very blessed to have this special bond with my son, not only while he was here on earth, but now to have this special relationship on a different level and dimension.

I have been awakened from my sleep by the feeling of a swish of wind going through my bedroom, and I find myself thinking of my son immediately. I believe he is there with me and wants me to know he is there when this happens. This feeling I get and changes in the air in the bedroom have happened to me on numerous occasions while sleeping. Sometimes I feel him brush up beside me or the bed shakes, and I awaken immediately. At first I will think maybe this is my husband, but then I realize he is fast asleep.

My brother Gary has been known to awaken me when I am fast asleep, but he jumps on the bed hard to wake me up, as he thinks it is a funny thing to do to wake up his sister. It is different than what Ty does. They are both funny guys! I bet they are both entertaining their friends on the other side who have also passed away.

Ty has brought my father to me. Never in a million years would my father have believed he could communicate with someone on the other side who had passed. My father was a bit confused the first time we were able to communicate through Marti. Once again, my son explained the process of how it works, and he got along fine after that. It did not take my father very long to catch on. Ty has brought many people to me who have crossed over to the other side, including Marc's father. Many times I am sitting in the backyard by the water feature Ty asked us to build for him. Ty always loved water. At this particular location, I get visits by family members who have passed. I asked Marti if I was getting more in tune with the afterlife or if Ty is bringing things to me. Marti said it is a little bit of both happening.

I asked Ty to tell Marti what I've been doing lately. Marti asked Ty, "So what has your mom being doing?" At first Marti thought Ty said I had been riding, like riding a horse. Marti has horses and I could see that she would maybe think that. Then she looked at me and said, "Oh, you are writing." I told her yes. She then said, "You are writing *"Ty's Story?"* I had never told Marti I was writing. It had been a little over a year ago when she asked if I could write *Ty's Story* and I told her maybe but not at that time. I was working at the time and too busy with work and just not sure I could accomplish this.

At one point during our visit, I noticed Marti's demeanor changed very quickly. I thought maybe she was either getting tired, as Ty takes a lot of energy from her, or maybe she was not feeling well. I asked if she was OK. Marti said Ty was taking her to a place she did not like and she asked him to never take her there again. She was hearing this noise like some type of machinery. After some time, she figured out most probably the noise came from a respirator. I could not think of anyone who would be on a respirator at this point.

I found out two days later after this visit with Marti that one of Ty's former band members from long ago, the band UnConquered, had committed suicide. He had done so on the same day I had seen Marti, but it was that evening after I had my visit with her. I have no idea if he was on a respirator before he passed.

My brother did not come to me during this visit. He isn't always around. Sometimes Ty tells me Gary is off fishing with his grandfather!

A great visit as usual to say the least. As I was driving home and got about a block away from my house, a red-tailed hawk flew over my car and followed me all the way home until I pulled into my driveway.

Saturday, October 18, 2014, at around 11:15 a.m., I was sitting outside and the telephone rang. I ran to the phone and once again there was a hesitation. I then heard, "Mom." There was silence and the phone then disconnected. This time the voice did not sound like Ty but more like my daughter's voice. I confirmed with Chanti that she had not called me. Could this be Ty calling me again?

Remember the wooden witch Ty and I moved back and forth playing games with? Well, after this last call that I believed was from Ty, I spoke aloud to him and said, "Ty, in the telephone call in which the caller said 'mom' to me, was that in fact you? If this call was from you, Ty, I want you to turn the witch toward the door."

Two days after I asked Ty if he had called me a second time on the telephone and to move the witch if it was, I got my answer. I woke that morning and walked to the entryway of the house and the witch had been moved, facing the front door.

It was Thanksgiving weekend, and Ty really was trying hard to get our attention. I was in our computer room, typing away, and I heard a crash in the hallway. I went to investigate, and Ty's picture of him when he was in the band, the Thoughts Killing Me, had fallen to the floor. There is no way that could have just fallen by itself, and I am amazed that the glass did not break when it hit the wooden floor so hard. Ty sure got my attention!

I had a small gathering at my house with some special friends who had come from different parts of the country to visit. We were to have a special reunion after not seeing some of them since high school. Marti was invited as a special friend to me and guest. We had brunch and Marti did readings for our friends here at the house.

One thing in particular that stood out during one reading was how Marti connected with my friend Gloria. Gloria had come from Erie, Pennsylvania, with her husband to stay with us. Marti said to her that she worked with people and liked helping them. Gloria is a nurse! She was right on with that. She also asked Gloria if she had a son. Gloria told her she did. Marti said she was going to have a granddaughter. Gloria confirmed that her daughter-in-law was pregnant and having a daughter. Gloria now has a beautiful granddaughter. Nobody knew that Gloria was going to be a grandmother until that day.

Marti talked about my son's former band mate who had committed suicide the month before. She told me that he placed a gun to his head. She asked me if that was correct, and I told her yes, he did so.

Marc and I were walking Yuba on a very cold day during the first week of December 2014. I saw something in the air floating down toward the ground. I stopped walking and stood and watched this object as it came closer to me, and I saw that it was a tiny black feather. We continued on our walk and a few minutes later a hawk flew right above our heads and squawked. It was as though the hawk was trying to get our attention so we would look up and see him. I believe Ty came to us in the form of a hawk, letting us know he was with us.

This feather reminded me of an incident that occurred this past summer. We were walking Yuba down this same street when there was something floating down from the sky. I looked up to see this tiny white feather, and I thought it so strange to be there at the time. This feather was within feet of the black feather we saw that cold day in December. That day during our walk a hawk also came toward us and flew up above us as we walked along our path. I do not feel these are coincidences. I believe we were meant to walk down this path at this particular time and see the feathers and the hawk during our walk. Marc and I both thought of Ty immediately and said that's our boy!

We had gone on vacation and had someone house-sit for us and watch Yuba while we were away. Our house sitter told me after we returned that during her stay at the house a young man appeared in the backyard near the water feature as she was outside sitting with Yuba. She had never met our son before, but had previously seen a picture of him. She told me that it was Ty who appeared in his physical form to her on this date. She said she was not frightened by this. It was almost comforting to her, though he was there for only a few seconds watching over Yuba and her.

On December 17, 2014, I awoke feeling very sad. It had been five years since my son passed. Even though we have this close connection, I was missing him so much. I have come to realize it will never change. Ty loved Christmas and always looked forward to being with family. He was a kid at heart, and I would tell him that he had to believe in Santa Claus or he would not come. All my kids believed.

I was about to telephone message my daughter Chanti, and when I went to my cell phone to send her a message, the phone went straight to my husband's messages, and there was a picture of Chanti and Ty. I do not know how this picture got to Marc's messages but it is a picture taken in 2007 on Chanti's birthday. This particular picture was e-mailed on Ty's birthday, August 5, 2013, to my cell phone. I have no idea how this could have shown up on Marc's messages and that the picture just popped up on December 17, 2014, other than Ty trying to tell me that he was thinking about Chanti and me. Chanti was having many health problems and maybe Ty was worried about her.

On January 8, 2015, I was talking to Marti on the telephone. We both spoke about life, hard times, and many things. Later in the conversation I told her how I was feeling kind of sad and depressed since the holidays and felt out of sorts. Since Ty's death, I do not sleep well, and lately I am having trouble with relaxing so that I can get myself into a meditative state. I explained that I felt Ty was pulling away from me. I did not feel as connected, and maybe I was asking too much of him. We finished our conversation, as I had to leave for an appointment. I got into my car, started to drive, and I got my sign from Ty. I had only driven a block from home when a red Fiat was driving toward me. I looked at the license plate and it read, "I'm here Ty." OK, I believe there is one extra letter on this license plate, and just maybe the spelling on the word "here" was abbreviated, I am not sure, as the car drove by too quickly, but this is what I saw. I believe this was a sign from Ty that he was still with me.

I have found in the past, when I am missing Ty so horribly, he always seems to come through for me with a pick-me-up of some sort, giving me a sign that he is still here with me. I went through the holidays as usual, seeing family, but I was missing my son, something that never goes far from my heart. I did not get my sign at Christmas from Ty that he was still here with me, and I was feeling sad. It was a beautiful day in Reno, and we were taking a long walk up the canyon above our home with Yuba. We had been walking for about one and a half hours when we came upon a bush along the path, and there was this one Christmas ornament attached to it. It was a small shiny green ball. It immediately caught my eye, so I walked over to it. There were no other decorations within sight, so I decided to take it; it obviously did not belong to anyone, as there were no houses there. I believe this was my gift from my son. This brightened my day.

January 26, 2015, I went outside to take a dip in the Jacuzzi by myself after having worked out at the gym. After about fifteen minutes, my brother appeared before me. He was standing by the trees looking at me, for what seemed like a few minutes. In looking at Gary, his form was more of a silhouette than what I see when Ty appears before me. He did not say anything, but I acknowledged him by telling him I knew he was there with me, and I thanked him for coming to see me.

These past few weeks I have received more signs than ever from both Gary and Ty. I just wish I knew what they were trying to tell me. When I go out to take a dip in my spa, a hawk usually appears shortly after I get in. The hawk will circle above me for about ten minutes, catching the winds high above until I can no longer see him. I have seen numerous license plates with various readings on them. I am feeling anxious and have not been able see my friend Marti because I haven't felt well. Hopefully, I will get some insight into what is going on with my boys and what they are trying to tell me.

Not too long after receiving many signs from both Ty and Gary, I found out that my mother was having heart problems, needed to have surgery, and would need to have a pacemaker.

Visit with Marti Tote on February 3, 2015

A very nice visit with Marti. It was interesting because both Ty and Gary were side by side almost the whole time I was with Marti. This has never happened before; they were almost inseparable. My father was very present also. He immediately began talking about a time when he had been on a train. Marti then asked if he was taking a trip, and he said no, this was when he was in WW II. So Marti said it must be a fond memory you had, and he said it was. I then asked my father if he was happy, and he said yes, he was very happy to have left this place.

At one point, while talking to Marti, I felt a rolling sensation from the couch underneath me, as if it was moving. Marti told me that no one had ever had that happen during a reading before. I was not really sure what that meant, but it was a strange sensation, to say the least. I said maybe Ty and Gary were playing a trick on me. Ty loved to play tricks.

Gary had been earthbound lately. I told Gary that I knew he had come to see me this past week while I was sitting in the Jacuzzi, and I thanked him for his visit. I first felt his presence, looked across the yard, and he was standing there watching me. He had also been so very present in many of my dreams. Through Marti he told me that he had also recently paid a visit to our mother. I asked if Mom was OK, and both Ty and Gary were quiet; neither said anything.

I had numerous calls where there was nobody on the other end, and the caller just listened to me. I asked Ty if he was calling me. Through Marti, Ty told me he had called many times, but he had trouble with me hearing him speak, as the vibration was the wrong decibel. He had to bring his energy level down and I needed to bring my energy up so that we can connect with each other. He said when he can get to the right vibration level with me, he can only say a few words. Ty told me that he heard my voice when I answered the telephone, but I was unable to hear him speak. Usually, when this happened, I heard a lot of static on the phone and a crackling noise. I almost got the feeling from

Ty that this was something so sacred for him to call me, and he was not supposed to let me into his world or know that he had this ability to do something so incredible. So you have to wonder if there is some higher power telling him no, you are not allowed to do this.

Ty talked about me getting a second house somewhere on a lake, and said that someday I will own another boat. I don't know where or how this will be accomplished, but I like this idea! He had brought this up many times in readings before. He does not think Marc and I will leave the Reno area on a permanent basis.

I asked my brother if he missed it here on earth and would he wish to come back, and he told me no. He spoke of liking his heaven. Those were Gary's exact words, "his heaven." I asked him if he worked where he was, and he said no. I then asked Ty the same question. He told me he does not work or miss it here, but he would like to come back to see me. He told me that it was a weird feeling for him when he "disconnected" from his body at the time of death. He said his angels were waiting to take him.

Out of the blue, my angels said my book is going to be published!

On February 13, 2015, I was talking to my son while walking Yuba—asking him why he has not been able to call me on the telephone. I wanted to hear his voice. The hawk was out. I could hear him, but I could not see him. After my walk, I went about my business at home, and I was cleaning the house. I heard a crash, looked around, and found that the wooden hawk that was sitting on my large television cabinet had fallen over. There was no reason for this to have happened, and I was nowhere near it. I believe it was Ty letting me know he was thinking about me and has not forgotten me.

I continued to receive many phone calls at the house and no one seemed to be there. My first thought was could this be Ty? I believe Ty was trying to communicate on the telephone, but it is a very difficult undertaking for him, as he has to bring his vibration level down, and I need to bring my vibration up to a level where we can communicate. I continue talking to him daily and asking that he call me or appear in his physical form to me, as I miss him so terribly. I believe this is probably a very difficult task for him to do, but he has done it before, and I know he can do it again.

It was St. Patrick's Day, March 17, 2015. I was feeling very emotional and could not really pinpoint why I was feeling this way other than I was missing my son. I was talking to Ty, asking him to please try to call me on the telephone once again, that I needed to hear his voice. It was a very mysterious kind of day outside with crazy cloud formations and a kind of eeriness about them. I went outside to read and have a glass of wine. I looked deeply into these clouds and remembered the day of Ty's celebration of life and how crazy the clouds were on that day. It was as if the clouds were angry. I looked high above into the clouds, and a hawk was circling. The sun was trying to shine through the clouds and had a large rainbow ring around it, mainly yellow in color. I stared above for probably fifteen minutes, looking at this beautiful sight, when I noticed a second hawk joining the first hawk. The yellow ring around the sun left and the sky had changed to a pink color. A third hawk appeared. It was as if the sky was a large rainbow.

The three hawks circled above my house with the first hawk flying high above the others. The sky had a green color among the pink clouds. A fourth hawk appeared. The colors in the sky kept changing and were the most beautiful I had ever seen. It was almost like having a light show up above me, and I sat there watching. There was a sense of peacefulness about me, as if I was one with the clouds, as if I could reach up, touch, and become them. I was sure Ty had something to do with this. It was like being a child at Disneyland without the noise and people!

One of the hawks was flying above me. The sun reflected on its body, creating a red-and-blue lighting effect. It was breathtaking as the hawk crossed up over my house. I had never seen anything so beautiful. I believe my son was trying to cheer me up, as it had been a rough one for me. He knows me so well, and he knows when I need to feel him and feel more connected.

I asked to hear his voice, but it is a very difficult thing for him to do for me. I know he will call me again when he can but he definitely gave me signs that day that he was with me. I am ever so thankful for that.

I was not looking forward to March 28, 2015. It was the weekend, and I had had computer problems for days; I was unable to receive any e-mails. I was expecting some important e-mails, so I knew that eventually I would have to take care of this problem. It was a Saturday morning and I just resigned myself to the fact that I would be on the phone with computer support for a couple of hours, and that was what my day was going to be. I was not looking forward to this, as I am not very computer literate. I called the help people, and you'd think you could get a person, right? Wrong. I went through recording after recording, not knowing which button to push. I got myself so frustrated that I finally said enough of this, turned my computer off, and walked away from it.

Meanwhile, there were other problems at home with sprinklers not working and such. I was having a talk with my son, asking him, "Can't you help us out some way?" A couple of hours later I went back to the old computer—and when I say old, I mean old. This was Ty's computer. I bought it for him when he was in college. I turned it on, and guess what? All my e-mails from the previous three days came up without my having to do a thing. Imagine that! I believe Ty had something to do with that one. Once again he came through for me and I thanked him for his love and support.

I had left to walk Yuba around 8:00 a.m. on April 1, 2015. Yuba and I had been out for about forty minutes and returned after the walk. I looked down at my watch to see what time it was and noticed it read 7:30. I thought my old watch was giving out on me, but I decided to reset my watch to the correct time and see what happened. Well, guess what? My watching is still working. I believe my son was playing an April fool's joke on me! My watch was working fine. Ty has always loved watches and had many of them. He has messed with Marc's watches over the years, turning the time on them, stopping them for no reason, and then, the watch suddenly worked again like magic. Ty is the magic! He always loved electronics. This is just another of his signs that he gives me that shows he really isn't too far away. Ty has never pulled this one on me before, but I thank you, Ty, because you are a funny, crazy guy who is just the same on the other side as you were here. I love you for it, and I'm glad you never changed.

April 24, 2015. Reno had not received any moisture in the air for a long time. But the previous night the rain poured down onto our roof so loudly that it woke me from my sleep. We so badly needed this. Yuba and I took our morning walk, something we do almost every day. I noticed that the clouds appeared the way they did on the day of Ty's celebration of his life. I spoke aloud to Ty about this and looked up into the clouds. They had moved in such a way that they allowed some blue sky to peek through. It was in the shape of a heart. I had just been talking to Ty, telling him how much I loved and missed him. Wow! If that wasn't something.

Yuba and I continued on our walk. I looked to the east, and I saw a beautiful rainbow across the sky. I had been upset lately, and therefore I made a wish. As Yuba and I made the turn onto our street to go home, I thanked Ty for such a lovely morning and the beautiful signs he gave me. At that time, I noticed the first license plate of the day. It was on a white van, and it read "KIDLIFE." If those aren't signs, I don't know what is. I am so grateful for them.

So many times I believe Ty tries to get my attention with the hawks. I will hear them screeching, and I run outside. A hawk will be circling above my house, and soon thereafter another will follow the first hawk, and the two will circle above our house. I wish I knew what he wants me to know, but maybe he just wants me to think about him or to let me know he's thinking about me.

Visit with Marti on April 30, 2015

I have been missing Ty so much. The days and years seem to go by, but you never get over missing your child. There is not a day that goes by I do not think of my son. I could hardly wait to hear from him and hopefully my brother Gary, too.

Our visit went well. Both Ty and Gary appeared almost immediately, as if they were awaiting my arrival. These two amaze me, as they both love Marti so much, and I am grateful for it. They are both so easy for Marti to read. They help me get through with life and make me feel happy that I can still have a relationship with them, along with other family members who have passed.

There was another man next to Gary, whom Marti did not recognize. She said she had never met him. She asked him who he was. He said, "Oh, hello there. My name is Jim. I need to tell you to tell my wife that her sister Mary is ill." This was kind of off the wall—like who is this person? Later, I spoke to my sister-in-law Cindy on the telephone, and she told me that Jim is a very close motorcycle buddy of Gary's who had passed away a few days ago from a brain tumor. I had met Jim on one occasion in Reno when my brother and his friends rode their Harleys up to this area. Gary told Marti he had many friends there with him. When I have these visits with Marti, it is like my loved ones who have passed have never left. They are right in the room with me talking to me. It is so incredibly beautiful.

I would give anything to be able to hear my son on the telephone once again. He has been trying on numerous occasions to call me, but I cannot hear him. I just get static noise and eventually the phone goes dead.

My dad came to me once again while I was having lunch with Marc. It was May 3, 2015, a Sunday afternoon. As I was sitting at the dining room table, I looked outside and my father was standing there looking at me. I could see his whole physical self. He was wearing a dark-blue nylon shirt with two pockets and white buttons. He had on light-blue denim jeans. He stared at me through the window, for what seemed like a minute or so, and then he disappeared. He did not speak to me, as he stood there watching me. I had the windows open, so if he had spoken, I would have heard him, but he did not. This was such an uplifting moment.

On May 20, 2015, I was writing *Ty's Story* and reminiscing about how horrible my first Christmas was going to be without my son. For some reason, I felt really sad and missed him more than ever. Some days are better than others. It's not his birthday or a holiday, just a day I miss my son. It's not easy writing about his pain and what he went through. I got up from the computer and walked down the hallway. Lying on the wooden floor was a Christmas tree ornament hanger. It was not lying there earlier. I do not believe in coincidences. I believe this was a sign from Ty that he was still with me, and he knew I was writing his book and thinking about Christmas.

I was on Facebook, and writer Lyn Ragan was talking about when you find a penny, it's fallen from heaven to let you know your loved one misses you. I went for a walk with Yuba shortly after reading Lyn's story and about five minutes into our walk, I found my penny. I also saw a "TF" license plate. So thankful.

Memorial Day came and went, and I was missing my family. Things were so different when Ty and my brother Gary were alive. I missed our talks on the telephone, our barbecues, and our times at the lake. Things will never be the same. I am still waiting for Ty's call. I believe he has called me since last October numerous times, but I need to hear his voice once again. I believe it's going to happen. There is a saying in physics, quoted by many that "Everything is energy and that's all there is to it. Match the frequency of the reality you want and you cannot help but get that reality. This is not philosophy. This is physics."

May 26, 2015. I was driving, and Ty gave me many signs, which appeared on license plates. The first was "ILUVMOM." I continued driving and saw a "TY" plate and then a "TFM" plate, "M" for Michael, Ty's middle name. I was looking at Facebook when I got home and randomly on the computer was a picture of Ty and his friend Brandon when they were about fourteen years old. I was almost in a state of shock seeing this, as it was the last thing I expected to see. A friend of Ty's had been reading our local paper, the *Reno Gazette Journal*, and posted this article from the newspaper onto Facebook. The article read, "We've added to our gallery of Reno institutions you'll never see again including the old Dome Theatre and the Del Mar Station pictured." The picture just happened to be of Ty and Brandon when they were in a straight edge band in the day. They used to play at the Del Mar Station quite often, but what are the odds, of all the pictures they have taken, they'd pick one with my son in it. I don't believe this is a coincidence.

I got up in the early morning hours of the next day to use the bathroom and get a drink of water. As I headed back to bed I noticed someone standing next to the closet doors to the left of me. As it was still very dark, I could not make out who it was who came to visit. I don't believe it was Ty, as the physique was larger. Maybe Gary stopped in to check on us.

I continue almost daily to see at least one hawk over the house while I am relaxing in my Jacuzzi, out walking Yuba, or driving my car.

On June 19, 2015, I was cleaning my house and talking to Ty, telling him that I was excited that I heard from his girlfriend Sarah after all this time and that she would be coming over to the house tonight and have dinner with Marc and me. It was approximately fifteen minutes after my one-sided conversation with Ty that my telephone rang and there was nobody on the other end. I suspected it might be Ty trying to call me again, but I could not hear him speak. Until Ty can lower his vibration and I can raise mine, it will be impossible for us to hear each other. This happened at about 9:00 a.m., and the phone went dead. Ty had told me through Marti that when he communicates verbally like this it can only be a few words.

I asked Ty to show me some sort of sign that it was he who had tried calling me. I asked that "Love Song" come on the radio or a song by the Beatles, and then I would know he had called me. Then I said to him, "I will make it easy on you. Just drop a picture off the wall or throw a penny if you want, just as long as there is no question in my mind it's you calling me.

I continued cleaning my house and approximately twenty-five minutes had passed when my vacuum started making a horrible noise. I stopped the vacuum, and there was a penny on the floor. I got my answer from my son. I thanked him for my lovely gift and said how special he makes me feel by his beautiful communications with me.

Sarah came over that evening, and we had a wonderful time. I wondered in the back of my mind if dogs (i.e., Yuba) would associate Sarah's presence with Ty. Yuba obviously recognized Sarah and was so excited and happy. It took Sarah a long time to get over her loss of Ty. She told me that the one night she did not stay home at our house with Ty was when he had passed away. I think she felt horrible guilt by not being with him, even though it was not her fault. I believe it was Ty's time to go, as he tried to tell me two weeks before that horrible day that he did not have long to live. I just could not have imagined it being so soon. I believe we all have our lessons to learn while on earth, and that when we have accomplished what we are supposed to learn and do, it is our time to go. Ty was an old soul and was ready. He was trying to tell me. Part of my learning and lessons while here on earth are to learn from my son and his passing. I am amazed how he has changed my life and what he has taught me.

I received a text message from Chanti that Isaac was playing baseball in Atascadero and that she had Isaac's sister Satori with her. It could be a long day if Isaac's team did not win and Chanti would have to stay in the hot sun until 5:00 p.m. The odds of Isaac's team winning the Arroyo Grande team were not very good, as the Arroyo Grande team was undefeated. Chanti was probably going to have a long day. If my grandson's team won, the game would be over at 1:00 p.m. for the day. Chanti had not felt so well physically herself, and so I asked Ty to please help his sister so she didn't have to stay out in the sun all day. I prayed to Ty to help Isaac too. Approximately ten minutes later, Chanti texted me and said they won! When Chanti was pulling out of the parking lot to drive home, she looked at the license plate in front of her, and it was Ty's initials, TYF. Awesome job Ty.

Marc and I had many signs on Father's Day 2015. We were walking Yuba and the first car that drove by us had the license plate "TYJ." Shortly, thereafter a hawk flew out of a tree from across the way, came toward our direction, and flew right above us. It circled once and then flew away. This hawk made a point of letting us know it was there.

Between 4:00 a.m. and 5:00 a.m. on June 22, I was awakened by a dropping sound. I heard it four times. It was as though Yuba was dropping a bone next to our bed onto the wood floor, and it was echoing throughout the house. It sounded very close. When I got out of bed around 6:00 a.m. and started to make the bed. I noticed three quarters and one dime sitting on top of the wooden bench that is at the foot of my bed. Ty evidently was trying to awake me, as he thought it was funny or just wanted to get my attention by dropping each coin onto the wood bench one at a time. It did all right!

Marc went to see Marti a few days later for Father's Day so he could have a visit with Ty. Marc did not say a word, and Ty, through Marti, said he had awakened Mom by throwing money onto the wooden bench in our bedroom. During this visit with Marti, Ty told Marc there was more money. When Marc came home, he looked around and found one more quarter under our bed.

Ty has also learned a new trick. Evidently, he loves to make noise, so he has learned to open my front door and slam it shut. He did this twice this week, two nights in a row. Ty also brought this up during Marc's visit with Marti. This even startled Yuba. The locked door just opened and slammed on its own or...

I receive several phone calls a week where no one is there. I suspect it is my son, and I talk to him. Sometimes I hear static noise and other times nothing. Just hoping one day he can get his frequency right so ours can meet again, and

I'll be able to hear his voice once more. Ty told Marc during his visit that he calls the house, as he likes the sound of the ringer. He also said that he can hear us, but we have trouble hearing him.

Ty also told Marc, "Wait until I play the piano." Still waiting on that one. I have heard some sort of music or chime sound a couple of times while inside the house, but I cannot pinpoint what type of instrument it is. Some sort of soft melody, and then it stops. I suspect it's Ty. One day I heard what sounded like wooden spoons banging on my wood dining room table. This just lasted for a few seconds, then stopped. I haven't heard that noise again.

Ty wanted us to know that we had a leak outside in the backyard. Marc explained to Marti that we had just repaired a leak in the front yard up on the hill. Ty was adamant that was not it. About three weeks passed after the visit Marc and Ty shared, and I was outside in the backyard. I noticed a slow water leak in the far back of our property. Once again, my son came through, only this time he was warning us. Luckily for us, the leak was not horrible and easy to fix.

Visit with Marti Tote on July 16, 2015

Once again I had a great visit with Marti. About a half hour passed, and Marti said, "Your son is here." Ty had a group of people with him. My dad had come for a short second, and then he decided he was going fishing. Evidently, this has become his new hobby since he's passed. My brother Gary was a no-show—sad, as I miss him so much.

Marti then asked if I had an uncle who passed because he was there. I said both my uncles had passed. Marti then said there is also somebody by the name of Jim. I told Marti that she had met Jim before. He is my cousin and passed years ago. Maybe it was his dad with him. We were trying to figure out which uncle was there with us, so I asked him to tell me how he passed; that way I would know which uncle was with Marti and me. He was so very eager to tell me how he passed. Immediately, I knew it was my cousin Jim's dad, my uncle Earl, who was with us.

I asked how he died. Uncle Earl said it was sudden, unexpected, and very tragic. Marti asked me if a vehicle was involved, and I said yes. My uncle explained to Marti that there were two other people involved in the accident and that it was his fault. Marti was quick to tell him that it was not his fault; it was an accident, and he did not intend to crash his vehicle. Marti then asked me if anyone survived this crash. I told her the other two in the vehicle survived. I then told Marti what had transpired that day. My uncle was forty-three years old when he died. He had been out with several friends and family members who all had four-wheel-drive Jeeps. They had all been messing around in the mountains, four-wheeling in the snow, when my uncle went off a cliff. The last thing he said was "Oh shit." Marti said to me that he was very charismatic, and his spirit reminded her of John Travolta when he was younger. She also said he was very handsome. I told her he was more like Elvis Presley. My uncle unexpectedly asked Marti if she liked him. I thought this was funny. He really liked Marti and did not want to leave. He hung around throughout our whole visit. Marti also told me that my uncle liked to fool around with mechanics and liked music, just like Ty. He also liked to drink beer. He said his mother was with him and that his sister was the last one left. Ty was around during this visit, but my uncle Earl did most the talking.

I ask for my son's guidance almost daily and sometimes I feel I ask too much from him. It had been so extremely hot in Reno, and we lost our air conditioning for two days. I asked for Ty's help in finding me someone to come out and fix our problem. I had made so many phone calls, and everyone was busy and promised to get back to me. Finally, I received a call back from this nice man who came out to look at our air conditioner. Yuba liked him right away, so I felt comfortable being alone with this man as he worked. Yuba is very protective, and he will not let people near me if he feels they pose a threat to me. As I was talking to this man outside while he was working, I looked up into the sky and saw a hawk above our house, circling. I knew then everything was going to be OK and that Ty once again had a hand in this, and I thanked him for his good work.

I was feeling low, as it was getting close to Ty's thirty-fifth birthday. So hard to believe. While walking Yuba one morning, I talked to Ty and asked him to please show me a sign that he was around. I knew he was, but I liked the reassurance. As I continued walking, a small hawk flew directly over my head. When I got home, I turned on the radio and "Love Song" by the Cure was playing. Ty knows I love that song. Later that day I went out, and as I was driving, I observed at least fifteen cars that had Ty's name in the license plate or his initials. This was more than I usually see when I am out walking or driving. I believe Ty wanted me out during this particular time so that I could see these signs. I definitely felt his presence, and I felt so uplifted by all the signs he had shown me that day.

On August 6 around 3:00 p.m., I was chilling, watching some television before going to my Pilates class at the gym. Suddenly I heard what sounded like something dropping directly in front of me onto the wooden floor. I first looked at Marc, and he was asleep on the couch, so I knew the noise was not coming from him. I looked at Yuba, and he was asleep on the floor. Geez, maybe it's my son! I believe he called me earlier that day also. My phone will say "out of area 1" when I get these calls that I believe are from him. I wish the caller ID would say "heaven" or something to that effect so I would know for sure it is him. There just has to be a way, and I am sure Ty will find it. I sometimes ask Ty if he is calling me to please leave me some other sign, so I will know he's calling. He does that by shutting the television off or turning on the lights, dropping money onto the floor, making things appear out of nowhere. He is so amazing.

As I am writing Ty's story, John Lennon comes on the radio, singing the song "Something." Imagine that? Ty knows what a huge Beatles fan I am. I just don't believe in coincidences anymore. There are so many things I have experienced over the years that make me believe my son is communicating. Either he is doing the best he can, or he is divulging limited information so as not to upset a higher power. I guess we will not know the answer to that until we have moved to the other side of the realm that separates us, and we can experience what he has. I am so thankful for what Ty has shared with me since his passing, and I treasure the visits we have together. I look forward to that day when I can experience the unconditional love and freedom he is experiencing.

We were getting ready to leave for our friend's house for the evening on August 15, 2015. When I got into my car and looked at the passenger seat before getting in, I noticed there were two dimes on my seat. Yep, my son once again left me a precious sign that he is around and thinking of me. I thanked him for his special sign to me.

Marc and I went up to watch two of our grandkids, Isaac and Satori, up at Shaver Lake this past week while our daughter did some writing for work. One evening as I started to fall asleep on the couch in the living room, I felt something touch my shoulder, but there was nobody there. Also, that night something bumped my bed in the night. It could have been Gary; he has done this before, as he likes to play tricks on his sister. He thinks it is funny that he can wake me up.

While up at Shaver Lake, nobody had been in my car. When I got inside the next day, there was a dime inside the cup holder in the front seat. It had not been there the day before. I believe this was just another sign from my son. Also, I saw many hawks flying over the house we stayed in.

On August 24, 2015, Yuba and I were taking our daily morning walk. I looked to my right as a hawk flew within six feet of me, landed on the wooden fence, and just sat there a moment while I observed it. The bird appeared to be doing the same thing, watching us. I love these signs. I feel so much love and happiness when Ty and Gary use signs to communicate with me, and when they do silly things.

Marc and I had gone to Healdsburg wine tasting for a little getaway for our birthdays, as our birthdays are only three days apart. The only sign that stood out for me this particular weekend was that two hawks circled over our car just after we had seen a license plate. I had commented on it, as it read "TYY." Ty is good about leaving me a sign, especially when it is a holiday or special occasion.

We got home and settled in after our trip. The next day, I received several signs from Ty. A picture of him, which is in my bedroom, had been turned downward. Also, I went to the bank the day, and as I was talking to a teller through a glass window, I noticed a dime sitting there in plain sight near my purse. I wouldn't have picked up this dime, but I felt it was a sign from Ty, as dimes are good luck, and I felt like I needed it that day. Before going to the bank, I had been talking aloud to Ty and asking him why he had not called me on the telephone again. It had been almost a year, and I missed his voice and felt very sad. Leaving the bank, I saw two more "TY" plates on my way home, which is only a couple of miles' drive. That same day I had been walking Yuba, and I saw a golden eagle sitting on top of a tree. A few minutes later, during our walk, the eagle flew right in front of Yuba and me, as we continued on our path home. When I see an eagle, I see it as a sign from my brother Gary, letting me know he is around.

One day in October, my telephone was not working. I could not get a dial tone to dial out. My phone would ring and my caller ID would say "out of area 165." A couple of minutes later, my phone would ring again, and the ID on my phone would say "area 1." I thought about this for some time and wondered if it was my son calling and it was a sign from him. The numbers one, six, and five add up to twelve and Ty passed on the twelfth day of October. I am still waiting to hear his voice again on the telephone, but it has not happened again. I pray one day he can call me again.

A couple of days later I found a penny in my dryer. I left to meet a friend for lunch that day and a hawk flew over my car. I looked up at the car in front of me and the license plate read "gutrplyr," (guitar player). I had just finished asking Ty if he had left me that penny as a sign, when I looked up and saw that license plate.

On December 3, 2015, I was walking Yuba and talking to Ty, telling him it was almost Christmas. I told him how I missed him more than ever and how much I loved him and blessed him. As I stopped, I looked up at a tree that had no leaves on it, and there at the top of this tree sat a large hawk looking down at Yuba and me. His coloring was such that he blended right in with the branches of the tree. It was so amazing.

On December 15, 2015, I was walking Yuba. There was still quite a bit of snow outside from previous days. As I was walking, I noticed a shiny red object underneath a branch that hung over onto the gutter area of the street. My first thought was that it might be my Christmas present from Ty this year. For the last couple of years, he gave me ornaments as gifts, and Marc and I pick out an ornament for him every Christmas. I walked past it, thought awhile, and said to myself, if it was from Ty it would be there tomorrow waiting for me. Just then, a hawk flew about twenty feet over my head and continued across the street—a sign!

The next morning, Yuba and I were taking our usual walk, except it was colder than usual. I first found a nickel in the street as we walked. We got to where I found the red shiny object the previous day and it was still lying there, so I picked it up and went along my way. As I continued to walk home, I spoke to Ty and thanked him for my beautiful shiny ornament. I looked up at that same bare tree branch where I saw the hawk almost two weeks ago, and there was the hawk, perched on top of that same bare tree looking down at me. I got my signs! For the last three years Ty has brought me to a place where I have found an ornament that was meant for me to take. He always amazes me.

A couple of days after Christmas I left for California to take care of my daughter Chanti and her two children, as she had major surgery. One evening I heard a noise that came from a stuffed monkey. Evidently, if you squeeze this monkey's stomach, it makes noise, but nobody was even near it to make this happen. We had been talking about Ty during this time. I then said, "Ty, if you are here with us now, speak up." My daughter said, "Oh, Mom, Ty cannot speak on command." Just then the monkey started making noise. That's my boy, always showing me signs in silly ways he is with me.

I am so thankful Ty is finally out of pain. His disease was such a rare autoimmune disorder. If you find yourself in a similar situation to ours, all I can say is never give up. There is always hope that some new cure is out there, or maybe somebody will listen. Now that's a novel idea! Though the system in our son's case failed him horribly, we never gave up hope, as there is always hope that the next day will be better or at least easier.

Epilogue

WHEN MY FRIEND MARTI TOTE asked me if I could write a book about my son, Ty, I was not sure I could do it. After some time, it came to me in a dream that I must get *Ty's Story* out, and I said to myself, yes, I can do this. I needed to do this for my son. I had to get his story out as it happened. He was a young man cheated by life here on earth, as no one would help him. He was a victim who was very sick, with no insurance and with doctors failing him time and time again. Even his own family and friends did not believe he had this horrible autoimmune disease called Behcet's. He was judged horribly during this time and became very much alone in his own world. This is *Ty's Story*.

About the Author

§

VICKI HAMM HAS LIVED IN the Reno, Nevada, area for over twenty-four years with her loving husband, Marc, and devoted dog, Yuba. Having lost a son has opened my awareness to life and death and has given me a broader understanding of why we are here. I truly hope that this book can help someone going through events similar to ours. Perhaps it will reassure them that death does not have to mean forever and that we will be together again with our loved ones.

Made in the USA
San Bernardino, CA
01 July 2016